QUICKBOOKS®
TOUR
GUIDE

Navigating Your Small Business
With A QuickBooks ProAdvisor®

QUICKBOOKS®
TOUR
GUIDE

Navigating Your Small Business
With A QuickBooks ProAdvisor®

Cheryl J. Graham

Niche Pressworks

Indianapolis

QUICKBOOKS® TOUR GUIDE
ISBN-13: 978-1-946533-26-5

Your Tour Awaits

Dedication vii

Thank you ix

My Journey To American Small Business xi

Chapter 1: The Small Business Entrepreneur Journey

    The Trip or Adventure 1

Chapter 2: Work Space and Workflow

    Dream Destination and Maps 5

Chapter 3: Accounting Method and Procedures

    Tickets and Boarding Pass 9

Chapter 4: Type of Entity

    Immigration, Customs and Culture...21

Chapter 5: Employees or Contractors

    Green Card, Visa or Passport 25

Chapter 6: Business Bank Account

    Travel Money or Foreign Currency 29

Chapter 7: Tax Agencies and Compliance

    Travel Security - TSA...39

Chapter 8: Marketing and Advertising

    Maps and Directions..51

Chapter 9: Customers and Vendors

Star Attractions...57

Chapter 10: Reports and Account Set Up

Travel Log or Blog...67

Chapter 11: Your Network

Travelling Companions...71

Chapter 12: Inventory or Cost of Goods

Getting Around - Rental Car, Taxi or Bus 77

Chapter 13: Filing System

Making Memories...83

Chapter 14: Profit - The Bottom Line

Home At Last...91

The Lingo...95

My Clients' Thoughts - Thank you!....................................103

My Journey To America 113

After The Tour 121

End Notes..123

Dedication

This book is dedicated to my parents.

My late father, H. Alan Magson, who achieved international fame from small town New Zealand, being placed 2nd in the world for ploughing, told me I could do anything.

Sadly, my late mother, M. Mynette Magson, lived half her life without my Dad. As a young girl, it was necessary for Mum to help raise her 10 siblings with no opportunity for even a high school education. Mum loved being a home maker and would "whip something up" at the drop of a hat to feed any large group.

She loved family and I can still hear her say, "If it wasn't for me none of you would be here." She had seven children, but sadly lost one at age 21 months, and I think even she would agree the rest of us turned out okay.

She never forgave me for leaving New Zealand. I had always planned on going back to live, but am sorry to say; it did not happen in your lifetime Mum.

This is a business book and I must say, "thank you" to my very first client, the late Billy Moore.

Without Billy's encouragement and support, my business never would have blossomed.

May you rest in peace, Dad and Mum, and Billy.

Thank you

I would like to express my most heartfelt thanks to all who helped me on this journey:

Kimberley and Stefanie

You were both there for me, supporting every new business idea I had as an entrepreneur. You never let me give up on my dream. The Three Musketeers. I am so proud of the women you are, and your accomplishments, in the business world and beyond. Thank you!

Michael

Love of my life, supporter, cheerleader. Thank you for continuing to encourage me, for reading and re-reading, and for helping me share my story. I am so thankful to have you in my life and my family.

Kathy

Thank you for always listening and encouraging me. Not to mention telling me to just get it done!

Karen

My client and friend; thank you for listening every week.

Ellie

Voice talent, actress, coach and dear friend, thank you.

Trina

Thank you for first introducing me to **QuickBooks**® and the world of American small business.

All my past and present clients:

You know who you are. I would never have made it this far without you, special thanks to Debra, Tony, Jayne, Rhonda and Mark, Anne Marie,

Sarah, Morgen, Blaine, Mark, Martha and Jim, Ernie, Eleanor and Mike, Cliff, Gloria, Jim and Roberta for your listening ears and advice. Thanks to Molly and Bernie too for your input.

To all the Accountants I have worked with:

Thank you I could never have done my work without you, especially Jeff, Leo, and Dale I am truly thankful.

Network Resources:

Human Resources, Insurance & IT:

Thank you Joe for your invaluable Human Resource advice and help to all of my clients. Thank you to Rob and the late Marcia for insurance guidance. Thank you Nate for always answering my calls.

Photography Team:

Ceara and Jen, what a great day, thanks for the laughs.

My book team:

Thank you for your unlimited patience Niche Pressworks.

Intuit® QuickBooks®:

Thank you for the ProAdvisor® Program – the support and encouragement I have received through being a Certified ProAdvisor® member has been invaluable.

My Journey To American Small Business

I am a New Zealander, affectionately known as a kiwi. I moved to America twenty-four years ago, it was the fifth English-speaking country I had moved to and I already spoke English. Although I had been employed as a bookkeeper and administrative assistant in the other four countries (more detail on that later), this was different. America was by far the most difficult in which to integrate.

I had so much to learn, from writing the date backwards (that was how it felt), to driving on the other side of the road, to learning a whole new vocabulary. American English is unique! It was November 1994.

My own name proved problematic, my parents named me Cheryl and I am one of five girls. My sisters are Alana, Lynne, Shirley and Sue. In age I am between Shirley and Sue, so we were often out together and to this day I can hear my mother correcting anyone who pronounced my name as Sheryl. I have spent most of my life telling new people I meet *"It's Cheryl with a hard CH."* No matter which country, but definitely here in America, I think people feel because of my accent that I am actually saying Sheryl. But no I am not. It is CHeryl with a hard CH.

I have adapted to living in America, but not to everything. My terminology and spelling might be a little different, but it is not bad grammar where I come from ☺. If you need help, there is a glossary of my lingo (terminology) in the back.

I learnt that "cart" was a "trolley," a "bill" (dollar) was money and what I had previously known as a "note," not to mention a " full stop" was now a "period," plus so much more.

I learnt that cart was a trolley; a 'bill" (dollar) was money and what I had previously known as a "note," not to mention a "full stop" was now a "period," plus so much more.

I learnt that everyone in America stops on the 4th of July and Thanksgiving Day even though it is on a Thursday.

INTRODUCTION TO QUICKBOOKS®

I am thankful for my wonderful neighbour Trina. It was the summer of 1996 and with two young children; she was managing their irrigation business from home.

She shared her small-business knowledge and accounting software that she used, called **QuickBooks®**. I liked this software and found it to be very beneficial for the small business owner. So much so that I decided to take some **QuickBooks®** classes and I continue to utilise the software daily, plus recertify annually, as a **QuickBooks ProAdvisor®**

AMERICAN SMALL BUSINESS

After a year, I was ready for the working world of small business with a green card in hand. My first job was with a logistics company.

So began my need to learn a whole new system, just as now you, the new business entrepreneur are about to learn a whole new world.

Through sharing my journey to America and American small business I hope to teach you some tips and tricks to use along the way.

I know what you are thinking…

"I know how to run my cheque book. I know how to check my balance online, so I can save money without a bookkeeper or a business manager and do it myself.

Plus if I buy that great software they advertise on TV, it looks like it does it itself, especially if I get the online version."

I hope you will consider seeking help before you go much further.

There is a lot to learn in anything new and you cannot begin to know it all at once. But just like me, you can do it! I personally hate to read the manual, so I have tried to make it easy for you.

So gather your team of colleagues to be a part of your journey and network; your banker, insurance agent, accountant, attorney and hopefully a bookkeeper. For the independent freelance entrepreneur working alone, this team is crucial.

If you are an American reading this, at least you will not make the first mistake I made, entering the date the wrong way. One full set of logistics invoices, entered incorrectly in the computer, entered as June 7th (6/7), not July 6th (7/6). From then on I kept a sticky note handy as a reminder to not make that mistake again.

You will have new tax deadlines and new business compliances and requirements, which you do not even know exist yet.

LET ME HELP

I love helping people with their small business and **QuickBooks**®. It is very satisfying to encourage them to become self-sufficient, confident and read the reports they were previously intimidated by. It can be so empowering.

With every new client I see the potential pitfalls for new business owners. Most of my clients are American born and raised; however I realised that the business world and all the compliance/regulations are very foreign to them.

My journey has been that of global travel and business, and as a result I have had much to learn, so I thought I would share that part of the journey with you too. However, first and foremost this is a business guide and as Dave Grohl says "Don't Bore Us, Get To The Chorus." For more of my journey you will find it towards the back of the book.

Allow me to share some things to keep in mind as you begin your new business journey and for those long term business owners, (or frequent flyers) some things to think about as you review your current situation.

MY FIRST CLIENT

My first client the late Billy Moore, voiceover talent extraordinaire, did what he did best and therefore trusted those who were helping him in an administrative capacity. As the business owner, he was unaware of the details of his bookkeeping going on behind the scenes.

In defense of those dedicated office managers and assistants who are trying, ask your employer for some **QuickBooks**® training in areas you are not so confident, it can make a world of difference.

Working for Billy highlighted some of the potential pitfalls for the business owner, but many I found challenging and actually came to enjoy.

Accounts receivable should be matched perfectly. Annual contracts should be billed appropriately with reminders set up, so no billing is missed.

I love getting the office books up to date and running seamlessly, so I can hand them over to the business owner or office manager. In this case I made it my mission to recover all the old **accounts receivable**. It took some time, but we did it.

It felt so good to have Billy's business in order and running smoothly. Maintaining it was easy after that. This was the start and I was hooked.

I want to help you, Mr. or Ms. Business owner or office manager, run your business with ease and confidence. More details to come later, but just a few initial questions of things to think about.

POTENTIAL PITFALLS TO AVOID

If you have a **merchant account** for accepting credit card payments, with a physical machine (rather than online account) check if you own it or lease it?

If you have a now "old fashioned" landline telephone at your business, look at the details of the plan. Was your price grandfathered in? Is it still current? Could you get a much better deal for less money?

Do you have a water cooler? If so, do you own the machine or is it rented? Check the rental costs versus buying.

It is rare that prospective clients find me when everything is going well. More often it is six months after they have started the business, and they suddenly think, *I should get that bookkeeping up to date.* Or it is tax time and there is a mad panic because they are not prepared.

GROWING MY BUSINESS

I added a film production company as a client, back when we still used the "One Write Check Machine®" and paper accounting system, moving into **QuickBooks®** later. This was a paper grid system with columns to total by hand. Keeping specific job costs separate was very important to match the bid or quote. Even twenty years later, I still have clients today who use the Kalamazoo® paper system and are only now transitioning into **QuickBooks®**.

Change is hard, I know. However, it is very satisfying for me to help business owners who have been in business for 40 years make a smooth transition into **QuickBooks®** from their old system.

QuickBooks®, the accounting software, works for virtually every business. However, the set up may need to be tweaked for your industry or your own company-specific needs. The key is in the set up and identifying income and expenses for taxes.

EMPOWER AND ENCOURAGE

Over the last twenty years, I have worked with over 200 clients in a variety of industries and businesses…realtors, churches, a translator, therapist, recruiter, bakery, auto dealer, painter, landscaper, recording studio, doctors, mortgage broker, plumbers and many more.

I often wished I had written down what I had learnt so I could pass it on to the next new business owner that I met. I am finally doing that! Just like starting a new business, writing a book has proved challenging. The learning curve for me as an author has been slow and difficult. Every time I read it, I think of something I forgot to put in. It is forever a moving target.

Now that I know you are reading this or listening to my voice in the audio version, I hope you will be inspired, empowered and encouraged to learn more and run your business with ease. In this book I want you to find the tools you need to run a successful business and read your Profit and Loss report like a pro.

As a bookkeeper, **QuickBooks**® coach and business manager, but not an accountant or CPA, I hope you will find this helpful and it will speak to you in terminology that you understand, even with the foreign twist.

The visual excitement from my clients, when they see where their money is really going and new ways to save and budget is fantastic.

The journey from New Zealand, to Australia, to England, back to Australia and now to America has been exhilarating and I hope you will enjoy the journey you are about to take with your small business. Allow me as your **QuickBooks ProAdvisor**® to help you navigate the business world.

Fasten your seats belts and join me as I lead you through what I have learnt on this journey.

Are you ready for take-off? Don't forget you can reach out to me…It's **CHeryl** with a hard CH and contact info is in the back.

CHAPTER 1

The Small Business Entrepreneur Journey

The Trip or Adventure

....

Moving from one country to another takes planning and preparation. Having the correct documentation, making a checklist and implementing it is crucial.

My story began with an air ticket, suitcase and a dream of adventure. I was young and carefree. It had taken much planning to get to that point; a long term job to leave, our house contents to pack, brand new furniture that had been for our prospective new house, all needed storage. Things fell into place for us, but there was no real plan after take-off; except a destination city to reach within a year, with some stops along the way.

My second major country move was like the first. However by the third country move and with a household to pack and two children in tow, the planning and organisation was a lot more involved.

Just like you with your small business journey, time for take-off...

....

Whether you bought a franchise, an existing business or took flight with your new idea or service, let's review your checklist:

- Business plan? **Check!**
- Capital funding or your own equity? **Check!**
- Business Entity? **Check!**
- Business Bank account? **Check!**
- Location or Office space? **Check!**
- Supplies? **Check!**

Ready for take-off? Maybe or maybe not …No matter what, you will want to plan ahead for a smooth journey.

As a new entrepreneur about to take flight into the world of American small business, you will find many resources available to you. How should you know which ones to take?

As you read through the chapters that follow, you'll learn from my experience of working with many small business owners, a checklist to keep in mind that might apply to your business, as well as some tips on how to choose the best resources to reach your goals.

I am a small business owner (perhaps just like you) and a bookkeeper. I am not an accountant, but I have learnt so much over the last 24 years in business, in America and will now share it with you. With every new client I wish I had written down what I had shared with their predecessor, as so much of it I repeat over and over. In an airport lounge in 2007, I decided I would write it down, but it never made it out of my computer. But now 11 years and 150 clients later I am finally getting it out the door.

If you are working independently, as I have done most of my entrepreneurial life, you will need your own flight crew; captain, purser, stewardess….a network of business associates. Allow me to be your first flight attendant and guide you as you begin your journey.

Remember; owning your own small business is *nothing* like working in corporate America.

I have seen it all over the years. It is rare people call me before they start their journey, but I wish they would.

If you have already incurred a flight delay or maintenance issue…in other words your business finances are already not as you would like or you are struggling to keep up. Get in touch with me now. My contact info is in the back.

In the next few chapters, we will navigate your workspace and workflow, accounting system, corporate entity, payroll, tax agencies, marketing, clients, reports, filing and the ultimate goal of the business owner, making money.

CHAPTER 2

Work Space and Workflow
Dream Destination and Maps

....

You plan for that dream vacation and you hope there will be no flight delays as you get to where you are going. A delay can be extremely inconvenient and very expensive. I remember waiting on our green card was nerve wracking, not knowing if we would be leaving or staying. Mapping out your plan is critical.

....

Your business space and workflow is very important and it's best to consider before you get too far into this adventure. Are you working from a home office? Do you have a retail space? Are you a travelling contractor who visits your clients? Are you working in the field by day, but coming home to capture accounting in the evening?

How will your work flow play out from the field to the office and how will everything be captured for accounting purposes? This is something to think about in the planning stages.

Missed billing is lost revenue.

Missed costs are lost expense.

I work in many different offices week to week, and each is set up for the business owner, so I share their space. We work together to develop a system that works for us, where their computer is situated optimally in relation to their desk or counter, work space and filing cabinets.

Funnily enough, when I work at many of these locations, I have dogs sit under my feet or cats sit on top of my papers on the desk, but I love the company ☺.

I have found if your files are not easily accessible, the chances of those paid bills or reconciled bank statements ever making it into the file cabinet are slim to none.

I am no exception myself and have my banking folders in a file cabinet to the left of my chair at my desk. To the right I have a hanging cart for paid bills and client invoices. The idea is that I will immediately file everything away, rather than lay them in a stack on the top.

These days everything is online or in the cloud. No one prints anything anymore, which is great for the environment, but sometimes can prove challenging for reconciliation. Saving a PDF works fine, especially if you have two monitors, but there is nothing like having paper files at hand to refer to and check off, if need be.

Electronic gadgets or devices like an iPhone®, iPad® etc. where you can access accounting software, might be an option for your business. The bottom line is that you need all your data in one place to invoice customers and run reports.

For those where electronic software or gadgets are cost prohibitive, having an internal paper form (template) or document, to transfer your data from the field or workstation to accounting is crucial. It might be a single document or a two-part or three-part form, but no matter what, it is something very important to keep in mind.

Calendars and scheduling are worth consideration also, as this might be the only way to track what billing occurred on a given day.

CLIENT PAPER DOCUMENT WORKFLOW

If it is just you, Mr. or Ms. Business owner making the sales and keeping the sales orders/receipts/invoices then that is fine. If it is more than you, you need a system to track this information, between you and your colleagues. Having options for growth will allow you to expand and not lose any data.

I have a few clients who have created an internal document for their orders. One client uses a single piece of paper and a copy is made after it is processed. Others clients have duplicate forms with multiple colours, one copy staying with the order, the other copy used for billing. These go to accounting to be invoiced to the client.

Everyone's needs are different, and I would be happy to set up a meeting to discuss your workflow, so we can develop a system for you. You may not have any internal forms but instead may add transactions directly into your accounting software.

One of my favourite types of accounting software is **QuickBooks**®.

See more about this in Chapter 3.

QuickBooks® offers three options to capture client billing and payments:

1) An "invoice" is how you can bill your clients. It suggests payment is coming later, with customisable payment terms ranging from due on receipt to any amount of days for your specific terms. Be sure to be clear about this.

2) A "sales receipt" suggests payment has already been collected, like in a retail sale at a store. More on that in Chapter 9.

3) No invoice or sales receipt. Deposit directly into your **QuickBooks**® bank account. With this type of deposit, you cannot track sales tax.

Some businesses do not require invoices or sales receipts or even sales tax. So bookkeeping can vary greatly depending on your type of business. More on this in Chapter 9.

....

In all the countries I have lived, I have worked in a variety of business locations. It is interesting to compare the space, environment and culture. The setup of your space is very important. When I was a courier in London for DHL my "work space" was my company hatch-back car. This was before cell phones and navigation systems. Paper work on the seat and packages in the back. Initially, when I started writing this book, my workspace was in an airport lounge, working from my laptop.

....

Capturing your data, whether it is income or an expense, is very important. Once you have your location set up, decide how you will capture the data. Mileage is an expense that used to be hard to track and I would have a log book in my car. I was not the best at filling it out though. Of course, now there is an app for that! But all expenses count in business, so make sure you don't miss any!

Your office space and how your paper work flows through it, plus the act of filing and storing files is important too. As I mentioned, nowadays most everything is digital, but some days you need physical paper to cross reference with an old fashioned pencil, rubber (yes we call an eraser, a rubber) and ruler to keep your line straight, to make notes on your paper. I have some great filing systems for myself and my clients - see more in Chapter 13.

CHAPTER 3
Accounting Method and Procedures
Tickets and Boarding Pass

....

Remember the days of paper airline tickets? When I left New Zealand I actually had a paper ticket valid for one year with stops in Australia, South Africa and Greece. So as long as I reached my destination within one year and continued in a forward direction, all was good. We had a plan.

....

Having a plan and accountability is key. Deciding on how you will keep your accounting is very important and often overlooked as you concentrate on your product or service. Oftentimes clients will overlook the accounting elements initially, knowing they can balance their cheque book. This is usually how I get many of my clients, once they realise it is a bigger job than they first thought.

With so much digital data and access online these days, many of my clients believe if they check their balance online every now and then, they are golden. I would beg to differ. Often it is tax time and clients have a mad panic to find someone like me to put order into their chaos. Do not confuse doing your taxes with a year's worth of bookkeeping. You need a year's worth of bookkeeping to have your taxes prepared.

You do not have to be a Certified Public Accountant (CPA) or even a bookkeeper to run your business. However, it certainly helps to get some advice from a professional before you start to navigate this world.

You will need a way to track your finances from the day you have your first business expense.

When you initially begin your business, finances may well be coming from your own personal bank account and possibly commingled with your other personal expenses.

Knowing where your money is coming from and how to code it for accounting is paramount. As the business owner you will need to decide, if you are **loaning the company money** or if that is going to be your **paid in capital**.

TRACKING YOUR FINANCES - options:

- Spreadsheet
- Shoebox of receipts
- Accounting software
- Word document

For tax purposes, you need to track expenses from inception.

In business a **Profit and Loss report**, and **Balance Sheet report** are the most common. These can be created using a list of your transactions. Every dollar you spend in every transaction will find its way to one of these reports.

At some point in your business, you will need these reports and it is good to know from the beginning how they are created and their purpose. Do not be intimidated, you can do this!

As I mentioned earlier there are many types of accounting software and I have used a few over the years. I personally favour **QuickBooks®**. A spreadsheet will work initially too, but remember your plan is to grow!

Also, without a double check of reconciling with your bank, the options with a spreadsheet are limited. That being said, I have seen a client with 900-line items on a spreadsheet and 20 years' worth of data. The transition into accounting software was much harder than they ever anticipated. But the reconciling element was virtually impossible without accounting software.

When you get that software, I cannot stress enough that **reconciling** your bank statement between the bank and your accounting software, is a must! We all make mistakes, even the bank sometimes.

Choose your accounting product wisely, while the commercials might suggest it is working in the background or doing it for you, I know otherwise.

QUICKBOOKS®

QuickBooks® can be set up to work for almost every business, but how it is set up is crucial, particularly the **Chart of Accounts**.

Before you begin the software search, check your computer for compatibility and space requirements. With each new software update, there are more computer system requirements for running it. Even your browser can make a difference. Check if it is a stand-alone product or subscription-based.

QuickBooks® is very user friendly, but it does not work by itself and does need data entry, editing and reconciling. It is a lot like using your cheque book on a larger scale; however you need to be conscious that every entry you make is finding its way onto your **Profit and Loss** report or **Balance Sheet** report.

CHOOSING YOUR PRODUCT

There are many versions of **QuickBooks®**, but the main three types (not including industry specific versions):

- **QuickBooks®** for a PC (larger version is Enterprise)
- **QuickBooks®** for an Mac®
- **QuickBooks®** Online (can be opened on any computer with the internet)

They are each unique with different attributes and there are different levels within each product. For example, the online version goes from the simple start to the plus version. Depending on what your accounting needs are will determine the best product for you. For example, if you need the capability to prepare 1099's or have inventory, the simple start version will not be appropriate.

It is hard to determine what you need when you have not really started transacting, so ask a professional for suggestions. If you look at the Intuit **QuickBooks**® website it will show a graph with ticks (check marks) in the list of options it covers. For example: track income & expense, run reports, estimates, manage bills and so much more.

Desktop PC **QuickBooks**®

- Robust sturdy product
- Single user can be loaded on Desktop and or Laptop
- Multiple user options available
- Home screen visual view flow chart
- Saved account setting options for vendors
- Bank download options if less than 3 years old
- Back up to USB or cloud

Mac® **QuickBooks**®

Only Mac-specific product *(unless you choose windows parallel or boot camp – to make your Mac work like a PC and install the PC **QuickBooks**® version)*

- Home screen visual view flow chart
- Bank download options if less than 3 years old
- Back up to USB or cloud

(Mac® **QuickBooks**® last product made 2016 - supported to 2019)

QBO® or QuickBooks® Online (becoming more & more popular)

- Data held in cloud environment
- Access via internet from anywhere
- Bank download options & auto connect
- Subscription-based product
- 3 service level options- Simple Start, Essentials, Plus

This is just the tip of the iceberg; each **QuickBooks®** version has so many features, check it out online: www.quickbooks.intuit.com.

Keep in mind, subscription-based products work well while you continue to pay the subscription and they will update continuously. However, should you decide to cancel your subscription, your data will only be stored for one year after the date you cancel. Alternatively, you would need to transfer the data to a desktop product.

QUICKBOOKS® ONLINE

Online QuickBooks® or **QBO®** is very compatible with online banking, but still requires connecting to your bank and matching the data to bring into **QuickBooks®**, just the same as desktop versions. However it is more automatic.

In the online version *YOU* must control the transactions, when you go through the "review" process from the bank.

Customer Payments in QBO®

Desktop users are familiar with receiving payments against invoices and that is definitely the best practice for **QBO®** too.

If you do not receive the payment against an invoice first, the online system will try to match to any open invoice with the same balance. You should be in control to be sure the correct payment reached the correct invoice.

Once you have **received payment**, (this is **QuickBooks®** terminology, but it could be both physically received and posted into **QuickBooks®**), unless it was your *"only payment,"* place it in **"undeposited funds"** to "deposit" with other payments. This way your credit card batch total or cheque total will match exactly the bank deposit, thus allowing the **QBO®** system to match perfectly.

DESKTOP VERSIONS

Desktop products need to be updated every three years for external features to work, for example – online banking and or the payroll add-on option.

Desktop single user can be loaded onto a desktop and a laptop computer, but only one location will have the most current version (unless you have network options). You can manually transfer data between home and the office via USB, if you have only a single user option, but the last file used will have the most current data.

BANK DOWNLOADING

No matter which version of **QuickBooks®** you decide on, you will need to download your bank data and manually edit it, so that it finds the correct account in your **QuickBooks®**. This is particularly important in the online version.

Regardless of the version of **QuickBooks®**, the system does not know which cheques you wrote unless they were prepared and printed from within your **QuickBooks®**. If that is not the case, you will need to edit the cheques at the banking import/review window.

I had a client once who thought because they had online **QuickBooks®** and online banking, the two would sync together automatically. However they were using a hand-written cheque book and outsourced payroll. So, all of that info needed to be manually added or edited (outsourced payroll can be mapped with a **Journal Entry**) to be sure it landed in the correct account.

CHART OF ACCOUNTS/GENERAL LEDGER

Once you decide on your accounting software and install it, you will have options for a guide to the **Chart of Accounts**, and the data created in these accounts creates your **General Ledger**. Every transaction you enter will find its way into one of these accounts. This same list of all the accounts will be used to create your reports, like **Profit and Loss** and **Balance Sheet**, once you enter transactions.

If you have an *industry specific* desktop version of **QuickBooks®** then it will also choose the **Chart of Accounts** for that industry. For example there is a Construction version of **QuickBooks®**. The **Chart of Accounts** can be added to and or edited at any time.

If you choose a *NON industry specific* desktop version of **QuickBooks®**, like Pro or Premier, during the set-up process it will ask what type of industry you are in and suggest accounts for your **Chart of Accounts**. These can be edited at any time, but initially this will be helpful. For example, it will label your income accounts based on the industry you chose such as hair salon, consulting, etc.

Often people come to me when they are trying to get financing or sell their business and the bank has requested **Profit and Loss** and **Balance Sheet** reports. They may or may not know how to create these reports, or if they do, the reports may not be in the correct format or have the accounts labelled in a way that meets the specifications of the bank.

ACCOUNT REPORTING TERMINOLOGY

Once, my client asked me to help revise their account names on their **Profit and Loss** report. Their bank had rejected the report due to the terminology.

For example, accounts were labelled:

- Business expense
- Cash-Debit
- Expense Account
- Loan
- Loan repayment

These are not well described accounts that an accountant or tax preparer would use, because they do not describe the actual expense. On your tax return you have specific line items that are considered tax deductions (remember I am not an accountant) such as office supplies, repairs, maintenance and utilities.

Based on the prior list I mentioned, these transactions may have been paid for with a debit or credit card, so they will be entered as a bank transaction in your register, but they should have an account code that explains the type of expense.

Using office supplies or auto loan would be preferable. The account name is important and will help identity the type of expense. You can create sub-accounts if you want to get more detailed, such as fuel as a sub-account of auto expenses.

It is not only the account name that is important, but the account type will determine where the transaction is found on the two main reports I described earlier.

ACCOUNT TYPES

For example: A loan is considered a *liability* and only the *interest* expense is a tax deductible expense.

The liability will be on your **Balance Sheet**, but the interest expense will be on your **Profit and Loss report**.

REPORTS AND ACCOUNTS

The **Profit and Loss** report shows three types of accounts:

- **Income accounts:** Revenue.
- **Cost of doing business accounts:** Direct costs to create your sales income.
- **Expense Account:** Overhead and other expenses.

The **Balance Sheet** report shows four types of accounts - Assets and Liabilities:

- **Bank Accounts:** checking or savings.
- **Fixed Assets:** Furniture and equipment.
- **Liabilities:** credit card balances, payroll liabilities, loan balances or sales tax.
- **Equity:** Money the owner puts in or takes out.

REPORTING FEATURES

Profit and Loss and **Balance Sheet** reports can be prepared two ways:

Cash Basis – income collected and deposited, expenses paid.

Accrual Basis - invoices prepared and or sent, but not yet paid. Expenses to be paid, included in the report, but not paid.

Cash or **Accrual** reporting and filing is set up when you do your first business tax return and cannot be changed, without contacting the **IRS** and/or making changes to previously filed tax returns.

However in **QuickBooks®** you can run your reports either cash or accrual. There is a preference in **QuickBooks®**, to set up as a default, but on each report you have the ability to override.

Know that your plan is to grow, choose a way to keep your accounting data that will allow the growth you are planning for.

Understand from the start that every transaction will find its way into one of the accounts in your **Chart of Accounts** and will be visible on one of the two reports I mentioned.

For instance, if a transaction that should have been coded as an expense is coded incorrectly to you the owner, it will NOT show up as an expense on your **Profit and Loss** report, but as an equity item on your **Balance Sheet.** If you accidentally code an expense item for a contractor to an income account, it will not show up in his or her **1099**. The detail is very important.

Reports are only as good as the data in them, so accurately coding entries is essential. Most accountants do not have time at tax time to drill down (expand the totals to see the detail) on your entries, because they will assume all totals are good. Most accountants will assume every bank account has been reconciled and transfer the report totals to your tax return.

If you give your accountant a report and one of your transaction entries is in the incorrect account, it is not necessarily obvious to him, without having the whole file or back-up information. Be sure to alert your accountant if you have areas you feel need additional review in detail.

TIPS AND TRICKS

In the desktop version of **QuickBooks®** one of my favourite tools is the **FIND** feature. It is found under the drop down of the EDIT tab, on the top line. I usually add the magnifying glass (FIND) to the icon bar in the desktop version, for quick access.

In **QBO®** it is under the **SEARCH** field top right. You need to select the advanced search in **QBO®** for more detail.

You can search by amount, name, date and so much more.

When your desktop **QuickBooks®** version opens up, it usually has the menu on the left hand side view and will be the generic navy blue colour. Try moving the view, to the top view, under **VIEW** on the top line; this gives you a bigger working screen.

You can change the look of your home screen, under **preferences**. I prefer the icons in a light colour, and the main ribbon colour (where you company file name is) to best match my client logo colour and a way to differentiate between files. There are multiple options found in preferences under the drop down from the **EDIT** tab menu, then select desktop view.

Also under the **VIEW** is an option for the **WINDOW LIST**. This gives you your recently opened screens and you can toggle back and forth. **WINDOW** also offers other options.

I recommend that if you have debits to enter manually and you do not need to track the bill, that you just enter as a debit expense or cheque (with no number). Entering a bill and then paying it is a two-step process. In desktop **QuickBooks®** this would be in a cheque format, but in **QBO®** there is an expense and cheque option, all labelled check.

MISTAKES ARE EASY TO MAKE

If you write a cheque for your accountant and you choose the account type "Professional Fees, accountant", that is where you will find that expense on your **Profit and Loss** report. If you accidentally type accounts payable, then that is where it will be.

If you deposit income into your **QuickBooks®** bank account coded to the account "sales income" that is where you will find it on your **Profit and Loss** report.

The data entry part is very important and at month-end and especially at year-end, "drilling down" (expanding the data to see what it is made up of) is so important and can highlight errors.

For business owners using a point of sale device that syncs with your **QBO®** file, check that your product and accounts match perfectly to make sure the syncing process is smooth.

QuickBooks® is great and with a few lessons you will love it!

CHAPTER 4

Type of Entity

Immigration, Customs and Culture

....

Anyone who has travelled internationally knows it can be intimidating standing in line waiting to have your passport or visa stamped, followed by Customs where you will be checked for bringing appropriate belongings into that particular country.

Since 9/11, restrictions are much stricter entering America, but over the years I have had many different experiences. After living in South Africa, I boarded a plane to the UK with souvenir African swords and a Zulu Knobkerrie (walking stick). I cannot imagine that being allowed today.

Travelling from New Zealand to Australia timewise is almost like going state to state in the US, but they are two separate countries with very different custom rules. You are not allowed to take fruit into Australia, and often travellers get off the plane with the apple they did not yet eat, only to find they have an expensive fine.

Since living in America I have learnt a lot about the governing agencies in business, primarily in Indiana, and the type of business structures available. Compliance and legalities are important.

....

CORPORATE STRUCTURE

You are about to begin your journey into the world of business and there is so much to learn. An accountant or an attorney can help you set up your **business entity**, but many may feel confident to prepare yourself online. Do your research.

From a tax perspective, it makes a world of difference what type of entity you select. A good accountant can share with you all the pros and cons of each, plus compliance for all the different entities. This is particularly important for a skilled and trained accountant, who knows your total tax history, both personally and professionally.

Sole proprietor, S corporation, C Corporation or Limited Liability Company (LLC)?

As an individual in America you can work under your social security number. This is referred to as a **sole proprietor** or you can form a **corporation** or an **LLC**. Either way you will need to register with federal and state agencies.

Although **C Corporations** are not so popular these days, it might be a necessary requirement if taking funds from your retirement account to start the business. So do your research.

Also there are different requirements from state to state. I have only worked for clients in Indiana, Florida and New York – so check your local rules before you start.

In the **State of Indiana**, the first thing to do on a state level is to register on the State Government website. This is known as **"IN Biz"**[1] and is a great resource for registering and managing your business, plus ensuring you are compliant with state laws. You need to contact the **IRS** for a Federal Tax Identification number once you decide if you will be a corporation or LLC and also a state tax identification number. Although initially, you may feel you do not need the State ID number if you are not selling a product or going to have payroll, at some point you most likely will.

I know some great accountants and I can refer you for advice.

Corporate entity? **Check!**

Once you have decided on your **business entity** type you will need a **corporate bank account** with the same name or if you are working under your social security, then a bank account for your business transactions, separate from your personal spending.

....

When I first moved to America, it was biggest culture shock of all the countries I had lived. So much was different; driving on the right, writing the date backwards (or so it felt), to many more nuances I learnt along the way.

When my daughters turned 10 they each had a Glamour party at our home. A lady was coming with a trunk of dress up clothes, make up and a camera. Before she could come I needed to get a waiver signed from every parent of every child attending? A waiver for a children's birthday party? Why?

Because the Glamour business owner needed to be sure if any child was allergic to the makeup the parents would not sue her. I had never heard of such a thing... so much to learn.

....

Just as I have learnt the American business way for the states I work in, you can too. Now on with the journey to the next few chapters…

CHAPTER 5

Employees or Contractors
Green Card, Visa or Passport

....

*As a New Zealand citizen under the age of 26, I could move to
the United Kingdom for 2 years to live and work as a local for the
experience. All I needed was a passport and a 2-year Visa.*

*It was a completely different story moving to the US. In the US, a
green card was required for us to work, and the entire process was
very complex. Because we did not understand what documents
we needed, we hired an immigration attorney for assistance.*

....

I would strongly advise you to hire an expert to help you set up your new
business processes and payroll.

Although there are many resources online for preliminary research, the
requirements for businesses can be difficult to navigate and understand. If in
doubt, search online. Search engines will be your new best friends.

PAYROLL

Should your **entity** be an **S Corporation**, you would be responsible for **payroll**.
This would most likely be you, as the **officer** and/or **employees**.

If you are going to have **payroll**, I would highly recommend hiring an
outside payroll company. They are much more affordable than you think,
because they process payroll in bulk.

It is not just the physical **payroll** cheques; it is all the taxes to various agencies, as well as the quarterly and annual reporting responsibility. The **payroll** company may seem expensive, but they are less expensive than missing tax deadlines.

There are a lot of online portals now offered through different payroll companies partnering with banking institutions that are very inexpensive. $55 per month is a lot less expensive than a payroll penalty and interest.

Federal and State payroll compliance regulations are complex, so acquaint yourself with these. There are monthly, quarterly and annual forms to be filed and payments to be made.

If you have accounting software like **QuickBooks**®, they too offer options for **payroll**, as add-ons features. This would allow you to do part or all of the payroll elements yourself or let them handle it all completely.

CONTRACTORS

The **IRS** has rules about contractors versus employees, so be sure you do your research. They offer a 20 point check list. Determine if you have employees and/or contractors.

As a corporate entity; LLC or corporation, if your company pays a contractor (not an employee), over $600 in one calendar year, for a service they provided, then you are required to send that individual a **1099** at the end of the year, unless they can prove otherwise. That is the law.

If you are using **QuickBooks**®, **a subcontractor** or **"W9" vendor** needs to be entered into your accounting software as a new vendor (someone you pay). In the Desktop version only, on the 3rd tab labelled tax settings, add their social security or Tax ID number, plus tick or check the box for 1099. On the 4th tab add the account code you want all their expenses to be coded to.

1099 VENDORS

There are 4 steps to capture vendor details for 1099's in **QuickBooks**®.

1. Turn on the **Preference** to allow **1099.**

2. Include name, full address and zip code.

3. Add Tax ID number and tick the box in the vendor profile to track **1099**.

4. **Map** your accounts.

When you **map** your accounts, you are linking an account type, with a **preference** to generate a **1099**.

For example you would **map** (link) your sub-contractor account to **Box 7** on your **1099**. That way every transaction for contract labour will be linked to Box 7 of the **1099**, provided you flagged (check box in the vendor profile) the contractor for a **1099**.

The combination of flagging the vendor and mapping the account will create the **1099**.

It is not only contractors that require **1099's**, consultants, landlords, attorneys do too.

Rent will be mapped to **Box 1** and **Attorney** payments will be mapped to **Box 14**.

You can create a report to check your settings are correct. It will show if you are missing any Tax ID numbers or address info. You can purchase the form **1099** from most office supply stores to print yourself.

Note not all of the **QuickBooks online**® versions have a **1099** option. The Plus version does.

All vendors who provide a *service* and are paid over $600 should be included, unless they are a corporation or other exception.

I encourage all business owners to collect **form W9** from each contractor when you *first* hire them – regardless of whether they are a consultant, photographer, cleaning professional, maintenance technician or whatever the service. That way you have their name, address, tax ID number and tax status on hand if you pay them over $600.

WORKERS COMPENSATION INSURANCE

If using **sub-contractors** be sure to ask for their insurance documents, especially workers compensation. If they do not have their own **workers compensation** insurance or cannot prove they are exempt, you as the business owner will be required to pay **Workers Compensation Insurance** on their behalf. Having certificates on file for your contractors could save you money later. We will cover more in Chapter 11.

HUMAN RESOURCES

As a small business owner you are your own Human Resources Department. So you will need to acquaint yourself with the type of documents your employees need to complete by law. There are multiple forms including an **I9** for Homeland Security, **W4** and **WH4** for federal and state withholdings. There are freelance HR specialists you can consult with.

Check the Federal website www.irs.gov[2,3] as well as your state equivalent. For those in Indiana www.in-newhire.com[4] & www.in.gov[5] are good resources.

If you are using an outsourced **payroll company** they will provide you all the necessary documents, but *YOU* will still need to submit the new hire signed form to your state agency. The **payroll company** will take care of all of your tax requirements as part of their service. **QuickBooks®** however offers options to include having the payroll taxes prepared or you doing them yourself.

CHAPTER 6

Business Bank Account

Travel Money or Foreign Currency

....

Every country has their own currency. There are all sorts of different shapes, different sizes, textures and colours. When you first travel or move, it is hard not to compare every expense with your home currency.

One of the most difficult things for me to do when I moved to America was grocery shop. Both from a money perspective, but also weights and measures, imperial to metric. In the UK, I was using ounces and pounds, but in Australia, grams and kilograms.

Once in America I tried to work out how much meat I needed by weight, in pounds with foreign currency, all of which is green. It took me forever to figure out if I was getting a good deal or not.

I also struggled with the nicknames for the coins - nickel and dime didn't mean anything to me. I needed to refer to them as "five cents" and "ten cents" in order to keep them straight. A quarter was a little more obvious and easier to remember.

....

You will need a business bank account and should keep it separate from your personal banking. If you are using accounting software you will need to get the information from your bank account to your accounting software.

BUSINESS BANK ACCOUNT

The IRS will send a letter stating your new company status and Federal Tax Identification number. This is what you will take to your bank to open your new business bank account.

The name of your corporate bank account needs to be the same as your tax identification company name. If you have a DBA (doing business as) you may need to check with your state to allow cheques in a different name to be deposited.

One step at a time.

Business bank account? **Check!**

Many of my new clients find me when they are confused with online banking and/or online accounting software. Their expectation is oftentimes that if they pay through their bank account online, their accounting software should automatically know who they paid, the type of expense and which account it should be coded to.

Downloading from your bank website certainly helps, but your accounting software will still not know the vendor name or which account to code it to, *UNLESS* you wrote the transaction from within your accounting software, printed the cheque directly from your accounting software, or manually entered the debit receipt. This is probably one of the biggest misnomers I come across.

RECONCILIATION

Reconciliation, reconciliation, and reconciliation

I cannot stress this enough. There is a **reconciliation** feature within **QuickBooks®** and other accounting software, please use it. When you match your bank statement with your accounting software it will highlight unidentified transactions and/or errors. I have had many clients who believed that the downloading and importing from the bank to the accounting software was reconciling, it is *NOT*.

Print your bank statement, (a paper copy), then if using **QuickBooks**®, select the **reconciliation** option from the banking area in desktop and under the Gear Icon in **QBO**®. Enter your starting balance from your bank statement. If you have done this previously in **QuickBooks**® before, it will auto populate, then add the bank statement ending balance.

If your starting balance on the paper statement, matches your **QuickBooks**® previous balance that is a good start. One by one check off all the transactions – deposits, cheques, debits and transfers. As you go through the process you will see the balance, between deposits and expense change with every transaction that you check off. The goal is to get "zero" difference to balance. Then everything will be balanced and **reconciled**.

Once **reconciled** the transactions will show in your bank register in desktop **QuickBooks**® with ticks or check marks for those transactions reconciled. If you are in the process of reconciling they will show as asterisk.

QBO® is unique, in that with the system linked directly to your bank and constantly updated, it automatically checks off transactions based on your starting and ending balance, plus the date. If it matches perfectly it is quite the time saver.

Once your banking transactions have been reconciled in **QBO**® they will show with an R (for reconciled) or during the process with a C (for cleared).

When this is done your accounting software will generate a **reconciliation report**. I would encourage you to print and staple it to your banking institution statement or at least save it as a PDF for reference, in case you need it later.

Reconcile monthly to keep good records and ensure your reports are accurate. This goes for all banking and loan accounts. Don't forget PayPal accounts too. When you make transfers between accounts, reconciling *ALL* accounts will confirm both sides of the transaction made it to the correct account.

Over the years I have seen a $300 cheque, clear the bank for $30. Banking has changed too; you can deposit cheques from your phone. But beware, I have seen the same cheque deposited twice and deducted from the payer's bank account twice. This error was only identified during **reconciliation**.

GETTING PAID BY YOUR CLIENTS

Cheques are old fashioned now, but they do not usually cost you anything to deposit. Bags of cash can cost you a fee, called a "cash deposit fee" for counting the money.

As the old saying goes "cash is king," but does require that you go to the bank to deposit. There are rules regarding cash deposits to business accounts for security and to prevent money laundering.

Just like changes to technology in the banking world; postage and communication have changed too.

....

Back when I first started travelling, communication was an "aerogram" style letter mailed. One piece of blue paper folded in three, sealed together with a postage stamp imprinted on the front. And - we only had land lines to make calls.

In 1983 I was travelling through an isolated area of the Transkei in South Africa. It was May 4th and my 24th birthday I had made arrangements for my mother, living in New Zealand to call me. We had to find a Post Office to take the call and our arrangement proved more difficult than we ever could have imagined. I remember taking that call in an upstairs office of the Post Office executives.

Fast forward to now, when I communicate with my family overseas on a daily basis. We can call or video conference with many applications and so many with absolutely no charge.

....

MERCHANT SERVICES AND CREDIT CARDS

Merchant services or credit cards are standard practice these days, as an acceptable payment method for most businesses, but all come with mandatory fees. It can be 2%-5% per transaction. The cost and fees to the business depend on which type of card was used. If it was a business card rather than a personal credit card that is used, whether it has points, air miles or other incentives associated with it – someone is paying for those perks! The business owner is paying those fees.

Now with merchant machines using chip and pin cards, it is a whole different world. I had an incident with a client recently, where a disgruntled customer had his chip card transaction reversed, because the chip reader was not used. The machine was malfunctioning at the time, due to missing an electronic update. So it was not accepting chip cards, and as a result the business swiped the card, and I am sure this still happens today.

I see it all the time at the grocery store where chip readers are not installed, although it has been mandatory for some time. The fact that my client's customer had received all goods and services three months before was irrelevant, and no amount of dispute made any difference, including the signed transaction receipt.

It was a technicality, but it did not help my client, the business owner, who lost the money. The actual transaction occurred in January, all goods and services were received. In March, without any warning, the total amount of all transactions was deducted from my client's corporate bank account. It's another reason to always keep your accounting software **reconciled** with your bank. You should always be watching your money.

Back in the old days, **merchant service machines** were generally leased for 3-4 years with a contract with lots of fine print. Many stated that once the contract was up, it was up to you, Mr. or Ms. Business owner to contact the **merchant service** company and cancel the machine rental agreement in writing.

It was customary to set up a direct debit from your checking account for the lease agreement. The person who set up the agreement may have been long gone, and or the contract may not be available, and there may not have been any reminders set up.

About ten years ago, I had a client who had that exact situation. Their regular bookkeeper was on vacation and I was filling in. I found a paper bill for the lease of the copier machine, but when reconciling the bank account, I found a debit transaction unaccounted for.

I called the 800 number on the bank statement and soon unraveled the merchant machine lease; which was three years past the contract end date. It was $30 per month, being auto-debited and the business assumed it was a monthly bank fee or rental on a copier machine. Watch your money – no one else will.

Double check the billing on your merchant service machine statement. Be aware whether the machine batches are "gross" or "net." The latter can create added bookkeeping. It is preferable to have your merchant company send the transactions to your bank in "gross" form and have the fees deducted in one lump monthly sum, if you have a choice.

Side note, just like **merchant service** contracts, telephone contacts can contain many hidden fees. Check your plan for the best deal.

PAYPAL

PayPal can be a good vehicle for payments, but the fees can be high and you still need to get this information into your **QuickBooks**® data file. Plus you will need to actually go to the PayPal website and transfer your money out of your PayPal account and into your bank. Then mirror (manually) this in your **QuickBooks**® unless your accounts are connected.

If possible, it is ideal to have your transactions run through your **QuickBooks**®. If not, you will need to enter after the fact. The system makes it very easy to write/print cheques and receive payments directly into **QuickBooks**®.

In other words if you print a cheque from **QuickBooks**®, it will automatically be in your software, as opposed to a hand written cheque that you would need to enter manually later.

DOWNLOADING BANK TRANSACTIONS

Manual Entry versus Download for banking transactions.

Downloading directly into your financial software can be a real timesaver. However, as we covered earlier, there are many factors to keep in mind when doing this.

Did you print your cheques from the software or hand write them? If it's the latter you will need to manually enter all information. Or you can edit and add data at the bank feed window, but not quite the detail you can on the *write check* option.

Remember whatever software you choose:

- Rules (similar to email rules) will need to be set up and trained for downloading bank transactions. It is advisable to add the "payee" or vendor name as you go. This helps the system learn which accounts to code which payees (your vendors).

- Cheques will need to be prepared and or printed from within your **QuickBooks**® software or added after the fact.

CHART OF ACCOUNTS - BANKING

We have touched on your **Chart of Accounts** and the type of accounts you are working with. We have talked about your **banking accounts**. If you have borrowed money from a lending institution you will also need a loan account set up in your **Chart of Accounts.** This will be a **liability account**, but it too needs to be **reconciled**.

If you have a credit card you use for purchases, you will need to set up a credit card account; this will also be a **liability**. This will also need to **reconciled**.

If you are creating an invoice, this will create **accounts receivable**. This is a liability account and once you have received the payment against it, this will automatically zero out the accounts receivable. You will then deposit it within your **QuickBooks®** bank account that you have created.

PRINTING CHEQUES

Printing cheques: If you print your cheques from **QuickBooks®** it will be easier to match with your online banking as they will already be within your program.

ONLINE BANK MATCHING

QBO® or **QuickBooks® Online** has just added a feature suggesting a **"possible"** match, as opposed to a **"confirmed"** match, when seeing exact dollars.

I have clients who pay multiple contractors the same dollar amount and the system would automatically confirm match by dollar, not cheque number, creating a mismatch.

The latest update to **QBQ®** has corrected this and now offers options for possible matches, for you to confirm. **Intuit®** encourages feedback on their products and many of the updates to **QuickBooks®** and **QBO®** come as a result of this. The online software is ever evolving and an improved version, from the one I worked with, when I did my first desktop file transfer in 2012.

I know I have gone over this but cannot stress if enough. If you are hand writing cheques manually, **QuickBooks®** has no way to know to whom you wrote the cheque unless you physically enter the data.

Online **QuickBooks®** and or bank feeds in the Desktop version will remember who you wrote the last cheque to and try to assign all of the other unassigned cheques to that vendor, if those cheques are not already in the system. This may be hard to understand until you have the practical experience.

I have many clients who use a bank "quick pay" feature. This is an electronic transfer from the business bank account to a vendor's bank account. It is not a physical cheque, but when downloading from the bank into the **QuickBooks**® file, the system can inaccurately assign almost all the payments to one contractor, completely missing all the other vendors. If you don't catch it at the time it can make the **1099** process difficult.

BANK RULES

Debit card entries will show up in your online banking, but again, can only be brought into your **QuickBooks**® register; if there are rules that point them to the correct account. The rules are like email rules, you train the system to put the entries where you want them to go. However in this case, the rules are within the bank feeds or bank review section (between **QuickBooks**® and online banking). At this point the system will let you assign each transaction to a specific account. Naming the vendor or payee will help for future transactions.

Remember, if you have multiple transactions from the same vendor it makes it hard for the "rules" to really work properly.

If you pay bank fees, a loan and merchant fees and/or transfer between accounts all from one bank, the downloading system has no way to define the multiple different types of transactions to multiple accounts, unless you train it to do so. I suggest you create separate vendor names within your accounting system and define each type of transaction.

FOR EXAMPLE:

These three transactions all need three different accounts, but are all paid to the one bank vendor. I would create three vendor names for the same bank with the type of transaction noted and account name to post to.

1. Vendor name = Cheryl's Bank Service Fees: coded to an account called bank service fees.

2. Vendor name = Cheryl's Bank Loan: coded to an account for loan principal and or interest expense.

3. Vendor name = Cheryl's Bank Merchant Fee: coded to an account for merchant fees (possibly a **cost of goods account**), but different from bank service fees.

As I said, I find the easiest way is to have different vendor names coded to the correct accounts and to train your download rules to follow this pattern.

RECONCILE, RECONCILE, RECONCILE

Reconcile your cash, I cannot stress this enough, and do it in a timely manner. This is probably one of the biggest problems I come across and really the only way to highlight errors and keep accurate records.

Whether your bank statement comes in the mail to your office, or you download it from your online banking website, print it for accurate **reconciliation**. Sometimes, even for me, having reconciled for my clients and printed the backup **reconciliation** report, I begin the next month and find the starting balances are off. It could be that a transaction was deleted accidentally. If this happens you will need to do some research to find the error throwing off the beginning balance.

Having the paper PDF **reconciliation** report is very helpful. I have had to create many years of data after a system crashed and the only way is through the bank statements to know what really happened. Banks can make mistakes too as I mentioned earlier a $300 cheque is scanned for $30. I keep copies of cheques, and attach bank receipts. Back up is always good. Reconciling is the same the world over, but currency is not.

....

European countries had their own currency until the late nineties. When I was travelling in the eighties, we were carrying multiple countries' currencies. One day the distance was similar to state to state in the US, and we were in Germany, Austria and Switzerland, all in the same day, using Deutsche Marks, Schillings and Francs.

....

Reconcile monthly if at all possible. I personally love to **reconcile**. I encourage you to always watch your money because no one else will.

CHAPTER 7

Tax Agencies and Compliance

Travel Security - TSA

....

When we first left New Zealand in the early eighties, the travel security was nothing like it is today. However my former husband had long hair and an earring back then, so we were stopped at almost every border control. They wanted to know about our destination, travels plans and to inspect the contents of our bags.

I do not know how many times I had to empty my cosmetic purse in front of a Travel Security Agency inspector. Or how many times they emptied the contents of our suitcase to look through it. We usually had to sit on it to close it again, but now in front of a queue of fellow travellers.

You may think American TSA is strict and it is, but in New Zealand they are concerned with the same obvious issues, but also as a small isolated country they have a great concern for travellers bringing disease into the country. Australia has similar added concerns.

You cannot take garden (plant) seeds from New Zealand to Australia. However you can bring them into America, if you "declare" them and they pass the US regulations. You can bring an apple into America, again you will need to declare it to customs, but you cannot between Australia and New Zealand.

....

There are so many different rules for different countries and so much to learn.

Business has its own requirements and compliance to learn and comprehend between the various tax agencies. Unfortunately, many people learn the hard way. Familiarise yourself with the tax rules applicable to you where you live.

Let me share a few things I have learnt regarding tax agencies:

- If you get a tax notice, do not panic. Open it and see what it says.
- Ignored tax mail only makes matters worse. Sometimes it is as simple as your tax filing was not received. Or the wrong quarter was entered on paper work.
- Follow up on all tax notices as soon as they arrive.
- Equally as important, do not just pay requests for payment notices without first checking the detail of the discrepancy. It might have been a math error, easily explained and no penalty due.

PAYROLL TAX AGENCIES

If you are doing your own payroll from your accounting software, you will need to know the tax requirements for employers.

Firstly you will need accounts with all the tax agencies. We touched on this earlier; you will need:

- Federal Tax ID number.
- State Tax ID number.
- State Unemployment account. The latter you can only obtain *AFTER* you have started payroll.

Payroll is not my favourite part of my work. It can be time consuming and is time sensitive, with strict deadline dates.

I encourage outsourced payroll, as it is very affordable these days and provides so much more than just the pay cheque.

But should you choose to "do it yourself" you will need to know important compliances, so check with your accountant and tax agencies.

When you do your own payroll, you are withholding employee wages to send to the governing agencies with your own company matching funds. This may seem obvious, but not always to everyone.

FEDERAL PAYROLL WITHHOLDING PAYMENTS

This is what I have learnt here in Indiana:

Federal Withholdings are most often due by the 15th of each month (exceptions possible), for the prior month and are paid online through the "Electronic Federal Tax Payment System or EFTPS", (www.eftps.gov).[6]

Payroll withholdings held from employee's salaries includes Federal tax, Medicare and Social Security taxes. These are paid on behalf of the employee to the Federal Government, plus matching company funds – Social Security 6.2% and Medicare 1.45% (at the time of print). The company portion is an added expense of your business and should be coded separately from the employee salary withholdings.

FEDERAL UNEMPLOYMENT

Federal unemployment is an annual *employer* payment, due by the end of January, although I have had a few clients who choose to pay quarterly (with their withholdings due on the 15th) or after the first quarter they reach the threshold. See the guides at www.irs.gov. At the time of print the FUTA (Federal Unemployment Tax Act) standard rate is 6.0% on the first $7,000 of wages, but employers that pay their *state* unemployment insurance in full and on time will receive a federal credit of 5.4%, when they file their **Form 940**. This results in a net rate of 0.6% here in Indiana. Some states have state loans which could affect the credit and rate. See the guides at www.irs.gov.

STATE WITHHOLDING PAYMENTS

In Indiana, state withholdings are due before the end of each month, approximately on the 30th, based on the previous month's payroll totals. If you are using **QuickBooks**® and preparing your own payroll, this should pop up with reminders in your **payroll liability** window.

In Indiana, **state payroll taxes** are paid online, check your local state, it may be a coupon to mail to your state. In Indiana you *DO NEED* to file the state tax withholding form **WH1** whether you had payroll or not (unless you have closed your account). The filing is a separate step to the payment.

The Indiana state form WH1 will include your **county withholding tax** too. You will need to separate out each county, or *IF* your accounting software is set up correctly, it will split your employee county withholdings. During a new employee set up, you will complete their local county tax information.

In Indiana the state and county payroll withholdings tax is totalled together, filed and paid together on the state website known as InTax (www.intax.in.gov)[7] website monthly.

STATE UNEMPLOYMENT

You also will be responsible for **state unemployment** taxes (SUTA) paid quarterly.

Each Quarter you will need to file and pay **State unemployment** (SUTA). The tax forms in Indiana are a **UC1** and a **UC5A**, which again in the old days were only sent by mail, but are now online or can be printed from **QuickBooks**®, if you have the payroll module turned on and set up.

FILING PAYROLL FORMS

In Indiana the **State unemployment** form is found at www.uplink.in.gov[8] - The Department of Workforce Development and can be filed and paid online. The state unemployment forms and fees are due at the end of January, April, July and October for the previous quarter. More information on Indiana State Unemployment can be found at www.in.gov/dwd[9].

Quarterly for Federal withholdings you are also required to complete a **Federal Tax Form 941** showing your employee Federal Withholding, Social Security and Medicare payments and your employer matching contributions. There is no reminder and this can be printed from **QuickBooks**®. It is due at the end of the month following each quarter: January, April, July and October. **Form 941** will show your withholding tax payments you have made via the EFTPS online portal and should not require payment, provided all payments have been made each month.

If there is no payroll, no monthly EFTPS reporting is required. However *filing* **Form 941** quarterly *is required* even if there was no payroll during that 3 monthly period.

Federal Unemployment Form 940 is due annually at the end of January.

I would encourage you to keep PDF or paper copies of all the tax forms you complete with the date filed or the date mailed noted.

OUTSOURCED PAYROLL

Outsourced payroll is looking pretty good, right? As I mentioned, payroll is my least favourite part of bookkeeping.

There are so many more options now with everyone online. If you do have outsourced payroll, remember you still need to get that data into your accounting software and it is best to enter it in the gross format.

In other words, without recreating each pay cheque, (helloooo, otherwise you might as well be doing it yourself), I can show you some short cuts that will get your total payroll into your accounting software and match exactly with your outsourced year end reports - **W2** and **W3**. This can be done with either a Journal Entry or 3 cheque style entries. Outsourced payroll can export a **Journal Entry** in some cases.

An outsourced payroll company can work really well when you realize all that is required for payroll and compliance.

For me, being at the computer with all the relevant data prior to deadlines can prove difficult, hence I like outsourcing. Just remember, you still have to give the time sheets to your outsourced company in a timely manner whether that be online or by phone.

See the following check list for most Indiana payroll schedule

FEDERAL PAYMENT MONTHLY	FORM QTRLY	WEBSITE	DUE DATE
Federal Withholding	941	EFTPS.com	15th
Social Security- Employee	941	EFTPS.com	15th
Social Security - Company	941	EFTPS.com	15th
Medicare - Employee	941	EFTPS.com	15th
Medicare - Company	941	EFTPS.com	15th

STATE & COUNTY MONTHLY	MONTHLY FORM	WEBSITE	DUE DATE
Indiana State Withholding	WH-1	intax.in.gov	30th
Indiana County Withholding	WH-1	intax.in.gov	30th

UNEMPLOYMENT TAX PAYMENTS	FORM	WEBSITE	DUE DATE
Federal Unemployment FUTA	940	EFTPS.com	Annual- Jan 30th
IN State Unemployment SUTA	UC1/UC5a	Uplink.in.gov	Quarterly - 30th

SALES TAX INDIANA	FORM	WEBSITE	DUE DATE
Sales Tax (Indiana)	ST103	intax.in.gov	21 or 30th**

** I have had clients with due dates of 21st or 30th

SALES TAX COMPLIANCE

If you sell a product in state, you will need to collect and pay sales tax. This may include shipping and handling, so check with our local agency to stay compliant.

....

I once gave fabric to a seamstress to make seat covers for me and when I received the bill for her services it included sales tax. When I asked why, since I provided the material and she provided the service, she explained that the state tax office had instructed her that thread must be grouped with the materials. In her business this required her to charge and pay sales tax. The point is to check your local tax code.

....

If you pay sales tax in Indiana, this will be due towards the end of the month following the month of the sales, possibly 21st or 30th. If you turned on **sales tax** in your accounting software and added your current rate, and schedule, the system will calculate taxable items sold.

You should review your **sales tax liability** report, to double check any exempt transactions are in the correct column.

In Indiana the sales tax form is a **ST103** voucher and our current retail tax rate is 7%, (at the time of print). Food and beverage industries have multiple sales taxes. Check with your local agency.

I have one client who has a regular customer out of state, and is required to file sales tax to that state. The state provides the payment voucher, in this case a paper voucher, to be mailed with the payment.

I manage a rental property in Florida where the state tax is 6%, county currently 1%, plus Tourist Tax of 4%. These are paid to 2 separate governing agencies and the state form in Florida is a DR 15 and includes the county.

For the Florida sales tax, we did start out with a coupon book and still could, but opted to pay online. Florida puts out their own schedule and each month is slightly different for the due date, between 17th/19th and 21st.

I have found some state tax websites are easier to navigate than others. Good luck and you will find my contact info in the back of this book if you need help.

SUB-CONTRACTOR PAYMENTS

Independent Contractors

You may hire seasonal help or other contractors to do maintenance, computer IT, graphic design, bookkeeping or another service you choose to outsource. These vendors are not usually paid through payroll, but as an independent contractor.

There is a government 20 point check-list to determine if you have contractors as opposed to employees, I would encourage you to check it out at www.irs.gov.

As the business owner using sub-contract labour, therefore not withholding payroll taxes, you do have other requirements on a contractor's behalf.

The tax requirements for vendors you paid for a service are as follows…

CONTRACTOR REQUIREMENTS – ANNUAL

Individuals, Sole Proprietors and LLC's will require a Federal **1099 form** by the end of January of the following year, they provided a service to you. You can read the IRS guidelines at www.irs.gov as there are some payments that do not need to be reported on **Form 1099**, but may be taxable to the recipient.

In general, as the business owner, you are required to send all your independent contractors, whom you paid over $600 from your business, a **1099 form**, unless they are a corporation. This is the total amount paid for services only in the previous tax year, not goods or materials.

The general exception to the rule is if they are incorporated. You will want your vendors to complete a **W9** tax form for verification.

Depending on the version of **QuickBooks®** you are using, and if you have the **1099** preference turned on, it should calculate your **1099** information. You will also need to include all Tax ID numbers or social security numbers and full address information. The accounts (contract labour or other) will need to be mapped appropriately. Otherwise not all the account detail will reach the **1099**, only those mapped. Refer back to Chapter 5 for clarification.

Note: *not* all online versions of **QuickBooks®** are set up for **1099's**.

The **1099 forms** can be purchased from any office supply store and include matching envelopes. You can order directly from the government for free.

There will be one **1096** form for the business owner to be included with the total number of **1099's**, highlighting the quantity and dollars of total contractor's payments.

The business owner will send this to the government with red copies of the 1099's (there are 5 copies of a **1099 form**) by the end of January the following year.

Of the five part form **1099** there is a state **1099** copy to be included with your annual payroll tax form **WH3** and **W2** state employee tax forms.

EMPLOYER/EMPLOYEE REQUIREMENTS - ANNUAL

If using an outsourced payroll company (which you know is my favourite), they will take care of your end of year payroll needs. They usually file and distribute your **W2's** and **W3's**, although some online services provide them to the business owner to print and distribute.

If you have any additional payroll benefits that were not included during the year, then you will need to get that information to your outsourced payroll company before year end so it can be included on the **W2's**. Examples include: retirement, health savings accounts, or bonuses,

As the business owner, it is your responsibility to have your employees **W2** distributed or mailed to them by the end of January the following year.

If you have the payroll module in **QuickBooks®** and your employees and agencies have been set up correctly, then you can print **W2** (annual employee payroll form) forms directly from your **QuickBooks®**. It calculates and allows printing provided the employee information (including county) has been entered in the employee section.

The Federal form that accompanies your employee **W2's** is a **W3**. If the **W3** form is printed from **QuickBooks®** it will pull the data from your payroll module, total number of employees and total payroll dollars. It is required to be sent to the IRS by the end of January the following year, including the red Federal copies of **W2's**.

The State form that accompanies your employee **W2's** is a **WH-3** in Indiana. The **WH-3** and the state copy of the **W2**, plus any **1099** information can be filed online at the Indiana Tax website: www.intax.in.gov.

INSURANCE COMPLIANCE

You will most likely need business insurance and **workers' compensation insurance**, the latter to cover employees and contractors working at your business location.

A good insurance agent is invaluable within your network to keep you compliant and tell you what you need. Your **workers' comp insurance** is based on salaries of officers, employees and contractors from the previous year.

Your broker or insurance company will send you, what is called a **workers' comp audit**. Ask your insurance agent or bookkeeper for help in completing it. It is a very important document and when completed accurately, you will be well covered by insurance and keep your premium cost down.

If you do not complete the workers' comp audit form, the insurance company will estimate what they think your payroll and independent contract labour costs are and determine your policy premium based on those numbers.

As I have mentioned before, if you are not watching your money no one else is.

CHAPTER 8

Marketing and Advertising
Maps and Directions

....

Back in 1997 I was approached by my friend Kathryn, an entrepreneur and woman business owner with a new internet company. She asked me to do the voiceover for her TV commercial for Net Direct, an internet provider, during the early years of the World Wide Web. The internet was such a fascinating tool and I do not know that we even realized where it would take us.

My script was as follows…

"Thinking about the internet, let's answer the question of which internet service provider to go with – right now!

With dial up access up to 56K and high speed dedicated or ISDN lines, Net Direct flies past any other service provider, in service and support.

And Net Directs redundant T3 access to the internet means you have a clean, wide, super-fast road ahead.

Steady service solid solutions.

Net Direct is your internet answer."

....

That was the new phenomenon back in 1997 and nowadays we tend to take the internet for granted and rarely print maps and directions. We rely heavily on our phones and online searches to get us to where we are going.

....

I was in London a few years ago, while my younger daughter was living there, and although I had lived there for ten years in the 1980's, I found myself using all the apps for walking directions and buses. Online is the way to go and the next generation will not know anything different. Yellow Pages – what's that?

....

MARKETING:

- How will your clients find you?
- Do you have a sign?
- Do you have a great website?
- The local paper advertisement?
- The local newspaper article on your business?
- Do you have social media?

You need customers and clients. You need cash flow; especially if you are buying goods to make products you sell in your business and paying vendors up front.

Social Media is equally as important as a traditional website.

Twitter, Instagram and Facebook are the norm.

The internet has come a long way from its inception and a well-designed website can make all the difference. However this must include good **Search Engine Optimization** or **SEO**.

Just like you want to do the bookkeeping yourself, spending a few dollars on a marketing company could make all the difference to having customers or not.

WEBSITE/ IT / SEO

Find a small business web specialist who will hopefully be a SEO whiz. He or she will contact the major search engines and get your company into the system with the Meta data (buzzwords to find you) most important for your business.

You may not feel it is in your budget to hire a web person, and you might be right, but the reality is, you can hardly afford not to. You need web traffic; you need people to be able to find you. Hire an intern with strong social media skills and it will make all the difference in the world.

If you have someone create a website for you, be sure to check if you *OWN* it. It could be subscription based and you will only have access whilst you subscribe to that company, and you may not own it outright.

Nowadays, how often do you open the yellow or white pages or even the online yellow pages. You just search on the internet, or ask an electronic device the question and they even respond with an answer.

NEWSPAPER ADVERTISING

Contact your local newspaper and any other publications that are specific to your industry and see if you can get an article written on your new company, sometimes you need to run an advertisement, but not always. Free editorial is the best form of advertising. So are reviews. I know many of my new clients have found me based on my **QuickBooks ProAdvisor®** reviews. So if you are reading this book and find it helpful, I hope you will consider a review for me ☺.

MAILERS

Advertising can be expensive so choose where you spend your advertising dollars wisely. People are always looking for a bargain; they save coupons. The mailers (an envelope of coupons) that go to private homes can be a great source for marketing dollars. There are online sites, like Groupon offering discounted rates for services. This might work for your business to gain exposure.

In my neighborhood we have a "Reach" magazine with coupons and advertising and we have a Value Pack mailer. For some industries these work very well, but for others it does not match their target market.

VEHICLE ADVERTSING

Vehicle advertising works well too for some industries, you can have your vehicle "wrapped" or have a magnetic advertisement to attach on your door or back of the vehicle. Be sure your phone number is clear for the car sitting behind you at the traffic light.

REFERRAL

A referral is the perfect form of advertising and endorsement; nothing speaks more highly than a recommendation from a previous client. Ask for reviews from previous clients, this works very well. Be sure to thank that client or offer an incentive; perhaps include a gift card with your thank you note.

BUSINESS TO BUSINESS – B2B

Another option could be to ask your local bank if they offer the opportunity to highlight a small business. Many do with a table displays, business cards, cookies, or goods, allowing you, their client, to promote your business.

NETWORK

Network! Even as the chief cook or bottle washer of your enterprise. Hopefully you can make a breakfast, lunch or evening meet up, as this will be invaluable. Take your business cards and work the room. Decide where you want your **target market** to be and hone in on that area.

If you are a landscape gardener….contact realtors, home owners associations, people who you know will need your services.

If you are an event planner, contact your local convention centres and connect with photographers, lighting specialists, florists and caterers, so you can piggy back off each other.

If you are an accountant who wants your clientele to be in the medical profession, then go to events where the doctors are or see if you can join their golf outing.

Networking and schmoozing works; small business is based on relationships and trust. If you have established a trusted relationship, when that person needs a service like yours, they will call you.

SOCIAL MEDIA

Facebook, Instagram and Twitter

I am a baby boomer and I did not grow up with social media, however I have had to learn and I am by no means the expert. If it is out of your scope of knowledge and you do not have millennial age children, as I said before, find an intern. They are inexpensive and knowledgeable in the world of social media and enjoy showing off their skills and talents.

We have talked about a few ways to promote your business and you will want to test them out and see what works for you.

BUSINESS CARDS

You will need business cards, there are many inexpensive options. Be sure your business name, service, phone and email are clear and distinct.

TARGET MARKET

- Identify your target market? _____
- Who do you want to sell to or service? _____
- How will your clients find you?_____
- Can you offer a referral program? _____

Would it be beneficial to join a networking group where you provide each other leads in your industry?

Depending on your industry, it is often beneficial to join forces with a couple of colleagues who work in a similar environment. Like I mentioned earlier, it might be good for a plumber to connect with a property manager or a real estate agent with a mortgage broker, so they can share leads with each other.

Promotional gimmicks can work too. Pens, sticky note pads, cell phone business card holders, the list is endless.

It might make sense to place an advertisement in your church newsletter or your child's show choir program.

Ask your new clients how they found you.

Once you have identified your **target market** and you have spent some advertising dollars, do an analysis to see if the promotion worked.

KEY PERFORMANCE INDICATOR - KPI

You will want to evaluate your **key performance indicators** (KPI's) to see what type of advertising works for you.

Sometimes it is a matter of trial and error. This is not my area of expertise, but I can refer you.

An accountant once told me, he gave all of his clients an Angie's List review form to complete, which he submitted. He was inundated with referrals from them, because of his high ratings as a result of the reviews.

Be creative, and keep an open mind, you never know what might work best for you until you try some different marketing options. Good luck.

CHAPTER 9

Customers and Vendors
Star Attractions

....

I had visited America a few times before moving to Indiana. My previous visits were to Los Angeles, Miami and Orlando, because with two little girls, Disneyland® and Walt Disney World® were both huge attractions.

Moving to the Midwest and landing in Indianapolis, the "Motor Racing Capital of the World" and being near the Indianapolis 500 track, was definitely a star attraction for us. We had watched the Indy 500 so many times on TV from New Zealand and now we were living here and visiting the track multiple times first hand.

My husband worked in motor racing which is what brought us to Indianapolis. My daughters and I spent a lot of time around many race tracks in America, especially the first year when I was unable to work due to the green card situation. I think we went to seven races in as many weeks that first summer.

One of our favourite races was in Wisconsin, at the Elkhart Lake race track. We stayed in the Siebkens Resort on the lake and the girls enjoyed paddle biking, tennis and the indoor pool when not at the race track.

We met great people both on and off the track and it was like a fraternity or family, all travelling around and away from home. There were many foreigners in the group and over the years we shared many a holiday together, all being away from our own extended families. Many of those wonderful friends are still in my life today.

Relationships are important in business too, building trust and reliability will help your business succeed. Look after your star attractions, your customers and vendors.

CUSTOMERS OR CLIENTS

Your customers and clients will be those you provide a service or product to, and the wonderful people who will pay you. These are the people who will bring you income. Your type of business may determine what you call them – retail establishments call them customers, while doctors and dentist call them patients.

In **QuickBooks Online®** there are a few name options for those who bring you income, such as customer, client, or patient depending on your industry. The desktop version label is customers and it is not an option to change currently.

If you are a retail outlet you will have a cash drawer or cash register, which may or may not be linked to your bookkeeping software.

There are point of sale devices that sync with **QBO®**. Make sure to check your settings on both pieces of equipment, to be sure all your entries are posting to the correct accounts, this is particularly important if you have inventory.

CUSTOMER PAYMENTS & DEPOSITS

You may just total your sales at the end of the day and enter them into your books as "shop sales". In **QuickBooks®** this could be entered as a **sales receipt** or directly into the bank deposit window. The latter will not track sales tax. If you are going to have a **sales receipt** for each transaction, and using **QuickBooks®**, the system will assume you have the money in hand.

An **invoice** in **QuickBooks®** will assume you will be paid later. In this case when your customer pays you, you will use the **QuickBooks®** feature **"receive payment."** You then will have the option to put the payment directly into your **QuickBooks®** bank account or group with other payments (**undeposited funds**) until they are all deposited in a lump sum into the bank. I am referring to both **QuickBooks®** account for your bank and when you physically take them to your actual bank. But the **QuickBooks®** terminology is **receive payment**.

A **receive payment** transaction could be cheques, cash or credit card. If it is the latter you will most likely have a batch time of day, where your merchant machine closes out all the transactions for the day and sends them to your bank in one group. Your **QuickBooks®** should reflect the same group of transactions in a batch to your bank account within **QuickBooks®**.

During the setup of your **QuickBooks® Chart of Accounts**, **undeposited funds** is one of the default accounts and is a current asset. The option to show your transactions going directly into your bank register is a **preference** you turn on, but this would bypass **undeposited funds**. It is best to use the **undeposited funds** account, unless all your transactions are single payments.

Undeposited funds is a **QuickBooks®** account that assumes your cheques are in your pocket or your purse and not yet in the bank. Credit card transactions that are in your merchant machine, but not yet batched to your bank account are also in **undeposited funds**. In **QuickBooks®** desktop version, on the home page has a great flow chart showing this and will have a red reminder of **undeposited funds.**

CUSTOMER INVOICING

We touched on the type of invoicing process you could choose in Chapter 2 and 3. If not using accounting software it can be hard to track who owes you money.

Will you invoice to be paid later or require payment on the spot? **QuickBooks®** offers two options - Invoice or Sales Receipt. Will you take a deposit in advance?

You have provided your service and you want to bill your client, so you create a word document with your logo on it and send it off. This works fine.

However it may not have an invoice number and you have no way of tracking who owes you money in **accounts receivable**, because without accounting software you have no computerised **accounts receivable**.

You would need to keep a list of customers and balances by hand.

QUICKBOOKS INVOICING OPTIONS

- **Estimate or quote:** a document for goods and services proposal, this can be sent to your customer to bid for a new job.

- **Invoice:** a document for goods and services that are complete and assumes it will be paid later. It can be printed or emailed. Using the invoice feature it will create a receivable for you to track when the payment is due.

- **Sales receipt:** a document for goods and services that are complete and paid for. This is a retail style feature that assumes you have the money.

As we mentioned earlier, the preferences in **QuickBooks**® come generic. The specific ones you need can be turned on or selected during the set-up process or later.

QUICKBOOKS VERSIONS

QuickBooks® **Online** version is being promoted as the way to go for the future. It certainly has some great attributes, and the flexibility to open your accounting program anywhere in the world, at any time, via the internet is a definite advantage.

The desktop version which has been around since the late 90's also has many great qualities and is a robust stable product that cannot be cloned in the online version.

The big brother to the desktop version is Enterprise, having the capability to manage large lists for customers, vendors, items or products and services.

QuickBooks® desktop users, myself included, often find the transition to **QBO**® more difficult, than those who started out with the online version. There are some unique features in the desktop version, not replicated in the online version. For example the memorized transaction feature is called recurring transactions in **QBO**® and there is no option for groups. The portability of **QBO**® is an excellent feature and hard to beat. There are other great benefits I look forward to sharing with you.

SALES TAX

We touched on sales tax in Chapter 7; again this is a toggle **preference** in **QuickBooks**® you will need to turn on. If you are selling a product to your customers, in state, you will be collecting and paying sales tax. Also, remember to check your tax requirements for shipping and handling.

You will need to set up an account with your tax agency and add **sales tax** as an item in your accounting software. If you pay tax to more than one agency, then multiple **"sales tax items"** will need to be created with the correct tax name and tax percentage value. Then, on each invoice or sales receipt that taxable item will calculate the tax.

The product or service you offer, if using **QuickBooks**® desktop, is referred to as an **Item** or **Service**. In the online version it is a **Product** or **Service**.

QuickBooks® software can be used for so many industries, but the set-up is key.

Let me share some examples:

A recording studio offers a recording session for $100 per hour, a **QuickBooks**® **service item** would be set up, and directed or pointed to the **income account**, in this case "Recording Income account." When this **item** is used in a transaction, the data will be automatically post to the **income account**, that it was directed to, and in turn show up in the totals on the **Profit and Loss** report.

The client also gets a **product**; let's say a compact disc (CD). This **item** includes **sales tax** and the invoice will be reflective of this, provided your CD **item** has the tax boxed ticked (or checked) and you have turned on the **preference** and added the current **sales tax** rate globally (throughout the **QuickBooks®** file).

The goods you sell will be set up as an **item/product** as **inventory, non-inventory or other charge item.**

QuickBooks® will hold the collected sales tax in a **liability account** on your **Balance Sheet** until it is paid.

NO INVOICE OR SALES RECEIPT REQUIRED

If you are a Real Estate agent you usually do not need products or services, and your income is commission. This can go directly into the deposit window in your **QuickBooks®**, but remember to enter the gross commission and deduct the expenses. The income would show up on your **Profit and Loss** report in your real estate income account.

We will talk more on this in Chapter 12.

....

Twenty years ago when I started with my first client, I opened his *QuickBooks® accounting software and pondered the paper work* *(back in the day, we did have paper work not PDF's). I began to* *realize that many payments had not been applied to the correct* *invoices, plus many annual monthly retainer invoices had not* *been created or sent. The challenge was enormous. Although* *at the time, I had a couple of other employment opportunities,* *the eccentric, bearded, talented man - the late Billy Moore and* *his business in his smoke-filled basement, somehow was a more* *appealing challenge than my other employment prospects.*

Seeing the state of his business; I was a little concerned as to *whether I might be paid or not. However, I had nothing to worry about. I made it my mission to invoice all the missed billing, collect ALL of the old collections and match every payment to every invoice. I was totally in my element; the challenge and the satisfaction getting it all matched up, and the day that final outstanding collection came in was exhilarating.*

I owe a debt of gratitude to the late Billy Moore, he trusted me to manage his business and I am proud to say that I did so until he passed away. His accomplishments adorn my office to this day.

....

CUSTOMER TERMS FOR PAYMENT

A few things to keep in mind about customers, especially new customers. Check how *their* **accounts payable** system is set up and if they require additional paper work. You will want to find out about their protocols and **accounts payable** rules.

- Do you have a contract?
- Do you have set payment terms?
- Do they have set payment terms irrespective of yours?
- Are your invoices due on receipt or is it up to 30 days?
- Does your due date start from the invoice date or the date the invoice is received?
- Do you email invoices?
- Do your invoices need to be approved before moving to accounts payable?
- Do you need a purchase order number?
- How will your customer pay? Cheque, cash or credit card?

Remember if you have not received a payment, it might be because you did not establish payment arrangements in the beginning. Or it could be because of any one of the following:

- Your customer needed a **W9** on file for your company and you have not provided one.

- The emailed invoice is lost in cyber space.

- Accounts payable department needed the sales department to approve before payment could be released.

- Accounts payable needed a purchase order.

- Accounts payable terms are 30 days or longer, regardless of *your* due date.

Remember, large corporations often have a much slower payment system than the average small business owner.

I have had clients who work with large universities and their **accounts payable** department requires their own set of documents including **W9** and other bank or business documentation.

CONTACTING YOUR CUSTOMERS ACCOUNTING

Establish how you will check on an invoice, via the sales representative or through **accounts payable**. It may be challenging when waiting on payment to find the correct contact phone number or email. Many companies today have only online support rather than phone support.

These are all important items to check with a new client so that you are not disappointed when payment does not arrive on time.

VENDORS

Vendors will be those you pay for goods and services to keep your business running. These could be large corporations or sub-contract labour for repairs or consulting. Either way, as we discussed in Chapter 5 and 7, if you pay them over $600 in a year from your company and they are not incorporated you will be required to do some extra paper work. I encourage you to request a **W9** prior to the first cheques being sent out.

PURCHASING BY ITEM NOT ACCOUNT

Something to keep in mind for vendors you pay, if using **QuickBooks®**; if you are keeping track of inventory you will need to receive your goods into inventory when you purchase.

In **QuickBooks®** you can receive goods into inventory with a *bill to pay* or the *bill may be coming later.* Entering the **items** will direct the transaction for the goods to **inventory**. Entering by account such as **cost of goods**, will direct the goods to that account and bypass **inventory**.

BILL PAYMENT VERSUS CHEQUE WRITING

If you enter a *bill* into **QuickBooks®**, you must pay a bill. It will have created an **accounts payable** liability and once paid will zero out.

In **QuickBooks®** you can opt to *write a cheque*, and the expense will show on your P&L, the same as entering and paying a bill combined. It is just one step, instead of two. Entering a bill usually works well if you have multiple vendors with multiple payment terms.

In the **QuickBooks®** desktop version this is found under the banking drop down or on the home screen banking area, labelled "write checks". In **QBO®** it is found under the plus sign (+) top right, vendor list, labelled "check."

VENDOR RELATIONSHIPS

Relationships and referrals are very important for those contractors and consultants you hire and can make a big difference to your business.

BUILDING & MAINTAINING RELATIONSHIPS

I am very fortunate to have maintained relationships with many work colleagues, clients and vendors, spanning 5 countries and over 40 years and I have found many of them a great resource for this book.

CHAPTER 10

Reports and Account Set Up

Travel Log or Blog

....

Nowadays you can blog about your trip or anything you do, or post it on multiple social media sites. Everyone around the world can know exactly what you are doing at any given moment. Back in the old days we wrote in a journal or trip book in "long hand" (with a pen or pencil) and mailed letters to keep in touch.

As I went back to my own "Trip Book" which I still have 36 years and 5 countries later, I made a discovery of the first cities I visited when I left. I had recalled that I left New Zealand in April and stopped in Sydney and Brisbane on this particular journey.

As I re-read my trip book, I discovered we left Christchurch, New Zealand on June 29th 1982 and actually went to Melbourne, Australia. Then we went to Perth on July 2nd, and after six months, on January 24th 1983 we headed to the beautiful island of Mauritius in the Indian Ocean, followed by Johannesburg, South Africa February 7th 1983.

I enjoyed re-reading my journey and recalling events as they actually happened and people in my life then, some that I have completely lost touch with, but am thankful for those 30 and 40 year friendships I do still have.

....

Keeping records to review later is only as good as how the data is kept or entered. As you progress in your business you will want to review your data to know how much money you are making and how much it is costing you in expenses.

CHART OF ACCOUNTS

We talked about your **Chart of Accounts** earlier; this is the list of accounts that is used in all of your reports.

Many people refer to these as categories or account categories.

Your **Chart of Accounts** or account categories will reflect the accounts your income and expense will be housed in, these accounts will create your reports. A few examples are as follows:

ACCOUNTING REPORTS

Income Accounts

- Service Income
- Product Income
- Sales Income

Cost of Goods or Cost of Doing Business

(These are the direct costs to create your income)

- Labour
- Materials (not inventory)
- Shipping, freight or delivery

Overhead Expense

- Advertising
- Auto

- Bank Fees
- Insurance
- Meals & Entertainment
- Office supplies
- Payroll
- Rent
- Travel
- Utilities

How the data gets into your **Chart of Accounts** is determined by each transaction, and that in turn dictates, how your reports look and the type of data they contain.

Some of the overhead accounts listed below could be considered "cost of doing business" in some industries.

For example:

- Malpractice insurance for a doctor.
- Payroll for a manufacturing company.

So it should look similar to this example:

Profit and Loss Report –

This will show:

- **Income amount** (dollars).
- Minus your **cost of goods** or cost of doing business.
- To give you your **Gross Profit**.
- Minus your **overhead expenses**.
- To show your bottom line – **net income**.

Balance Sheet Report –

This will show your assets and liabilities:

- Bank Accounts.
- Assets-value of assets owned by your company, including vehicles and buildings.
- Liabilities – loans, credit card balances, accounts receivable and payable.
- Equity- paid in capital or monies put in and out by the owner.

SALES REPORTS

For sales reports these can be created based on your accounts and/or items and products. It all depends on the way the items were set-up and how your data is entered.

QuickBooks® offers many sales reporting features, but it is all determined on how the data was entered, per client or per job, or per item or product.

For example if you want to know how many red t shirts, size large you sold; but you only entered them as large t shirts with no colour noted, you will not be able to create a report to show that.

QUICKBOOKS® END OF YEAR REPORTING

QuickBooks® has a built in feature and at the beginning of a new year it will automatically transfer your net income to your retained earnings account from the prior fiscal year.

Your fiscal year is your accounting tax year and may not be a calendar year. **QuickBooks®** *DOES NOT transfer* your shareholder or owner distributions, so you will need to do this yourself or ask your accountant or bookkeeper. This **journal entry** will be dated the first of the next fiscal year.

CREDIT – Distributions

DEBIT – Retained Earnings

CHAPTER 11
Your Network
Travelling Companions

....

It took me a long time to integrate into America; I was very lonely and found the culture very different and difficult. In the community we moved into, Zionsville, Indiana, locals assumed because I spoke English, that I knew how the system worked, but I did not. I didn't know the tax system, the bank system, the school system, the medical system, the health insurance system and many, many more. I needed to make friends and learn these new systems.

We arrived on November 30th 1994. My girls had been in year round school in Australia, and would have been having their 6-week summer holiday beginning mid-December, instead were in a new country starting winter.

My daughters (almost 7 and 9) were going to wait until after the New Year to start American school. However, they were bored inside during the winter, and not knowing anyone, so started school mid-December. Then they had Christmas break and returned for the New Year.

The first day for me, putting them on the bus for the first time (I had always taken them to school and walked them into their classrooms to greet the teacher) and watching that yellow bus drive away was very difficult. I know it was hard for them too. The other children teased them for their accents and for the first time, they had to go to separate schools all by themselves. I will never forget that day walking back to our rented home with tears in my eyes, after putting them on the bus. Change is hard.

In the Australian school the girls had attended, the children primarily brought their lunch from home and all ate outdoors. They had a snack shop, but not a cafeteria. Playtime was for playing on the equipment provided. Recess here in the US was very different.

In February 1995 my older daughter Kim, was in a large group class - 3 teachers and 3 groups of students, 70 children in all. Kim came home and said she needed 70 Valentines cards? How could that be? "I Love You" at $5 apiece and you need 70, there must be some mistake. Yes there was! Then I learnt that for Valentine's Day in America children can buy a themed box of 20 cards, including one for the teacher. This was new and novel.

The girls were always getting their spelling wrong at school, and I was not much help. Clearly we spelt words differently and had to learn a whole new English vocabulary and spelling. We failed at the homophones too, because with our accents we said words differently. Americans struggled to hear the difference when we said Bob or Barb, or pasta and pastor.

Over time the girls made wonderful friends at school and many lifelong friends. I was fortunate to make friends with many of their parents. However, building my business network took me much longer, as I waited on my Green Card and work visa.

....

Change is hard and small business is *nothing* like corporate America with work colleagues who congregate at the water cooler or get together after work.

So, arm yourself with a good group of friends or travelling companions as you make this journey into business. Call on resources to help you learn the systems to make your transition into entrepreneurship easier and smooth.

TRAVELLNG COMPANIONS

The Travelling Companions for your business journey I would recommend:

Accountant and Bookkeeper: I am very fortunate to have created wonderful working friendships with many accountants and have found them to be an amazing resource for both myself and my clients. I find the smaller firms best for most of my clients.

Think about what your needs are. Do you need an accountant with a boardroom and an assistant or would you be okay with a one-man band working from home?

Banker: You will need to open a business bank account. Find out who your private banker is, as they will be invaluable.

Human Resources: Keep current with human resource, compliance can be difficult to navigate. Finding a freelance HR representative who can help with employee manuals and compliance guidelines will be a great asset.

Insurance Agent: You will need a good insurance agent; they will tell you what you need for your industry and keep you compliant, plus save you money.

....

I had a new client who had not completed a workers comp audit form, these are usually sent annually prior to the renewal date. They did not know what it was and had ignored it. If an insurance audit is not completed and returned, the insurance company will be forced to estimate your premium, based on estimates of your payroll and contractor amounts paid. This could mean your workers comp premium is much higher than it needs to be. The premium price is determined by wages and contractor expenses from the previous year. This is what happened to my client and their premiums were exorbitant and grossly overpriced.

I was there to help teach and train **QuickBooks®** *and reconciliation. But during that process I noticed their insurance was very high and started reviewing their payroll and it did not seem consistent with the type of workers comp insurance fees.*

My broker, the late Marcia Baker, had taught me a sense of how to gauge these, but she was my rock, so I called her and she gave me good insight. With further investigation, we discovered the rates were incorrect due to the audit not being completed.

With the help of my client's insurance broker I was able to get the premiums corrected, retroactively with a large refund. My client shared a very nice testimonial you can read towards the back of this book.

....

Printer: I also have a great printer that I work with locally here in Indianapolis and although you can order almost everything online. Check out the local printers in your area, they may be a small business just like you. I have utilised Writeguard Business System (www.writeguard.com) for myself and many of my clients. Business cards, 3 part cheques, personalised forms in duplicate and triplicate, and so much more.

NETWORK WITH YOUR TRAVELLING COMPANIONS

Join Network Groups:

- BNI (Business Network International)
- Referral Key
- Meet Ups

For Women and Minority Groups:

- WBE – Women Business Enterprise
- WBENC – Women Business National Council
- NAWBO – National Association of Women Business Owners

Another great group to connect with for help and guidance through the US based Small Business Association, is SCORE. This group of retired business men and women are excellent mentors.

These will be invaluable to help grow your network of colleagues, customers and vendors.

As you build your network you will refer colleagues you have met to others. If you find you are the recipient of a referral, be sure to acknowledge it. Send them a thank you card or email or gift card to express your appreciation.

I love to network and when I meet someone new, I am always thinking of others in my rolodex (an old fashioned business card holder of contacts) that would make a good connection. As I mentioned earlier, I am thankful for the work colleagues of 30 and 40 years still in my network.

CHAPTER 12

Inventory or Cost of Goods

Getting Around - Rental Car, Taxi or Bus

....

Planes, trains and automobiles that is what it used to be. But now we have Uber® and Lfyt® and many other options to navigate our surroundings. We do not always need to use hotels anymore. We can stay at stranger's private homes through Airbnb®.

I have shared with you how hard it was for me to navigate the systems and integrate into the culture when my family and I moved to the US.

....

The same can be said of small business regarding decisions on **cost of goods** versus **inventory**. Should you use **cost of goods** for the materials you sell or are they **inventory**?

This can pose problems if not set up correctly in the first place. **Inventory** suggests you own materials stored at your location, which is an **asset account** (in your **Chart of Accounts**) and the value will be used to calculate your **Business Tangible tax**.

Cost of goods suggests you buy materials to pass on to your clients, but technically you do not keep in stock or on hand. This account type is a **cost of goods** type expense account.

Cost of goods shows up on your **Profit and Loss** report, but above your overhead expense.

Inventory could run through your **Cost of Goods**, but it is an **asset** of your company and, as an **asset** shows up on your **Balance Sheet** until the goods are sold.

INVENTORY OR COST OF GOODS

If you sell a product rather than offer a service, you will need to decide how your goods or materials are coming into and going out of your business, from an accounting perspective.

The terminology of **QuickBooks®** for goods and materials is called either an **item** or a **product**, depending on which version you are using.

In the **QuickBooks®** Desktop version you would be creating an **Item** for your goods or materials.

In the **QuickBooks®** Online version you would be creating a **Product**.

NAME	TYPE	ACCOUNT
Item or Product	Inventory	Asset Account (Inventory)
Item or Product	Non-Inventory	Cost of Goods Account
Shipping	Other charge	Cost Of Goods Shipping Account

The account type is very important and this makes a big difference to your accounting. Will it be an **inventory** part therefore an **asset** or a **cost of goods** therefore an expense.

This can be tricky.

If you buy a product to sell and keep it "in house," it will most likely be considered an **inventory item**. This would be an asset of your company and the value will be on your **Balance Sheet**. The value will be a consideration for both **business tangible taxes** and on your tax return at the end of year.

If it is **inventory** and an **asset**, you should have set up a **double sided item**, (this is **QuickBooks**® terminology). If it is set up correctly, the item should flow through your **cost of goods** when sold. Your **inventory** will be reduced both by quantity and value of the asset. So, until the item is sold it is an **asset** of your company and its value is on your **Balance Sheet**.

In **QuickBooks**®, if you are not already confused or overwhelmed (to add another layer), items that are **double sided** show both expense account and income account.

If you set up an **inventory item** this will show the **inventory asset** account too. One side of the **item** is used when you enter the purchase and the other when you enter the sale.

If you buy a product to pass on to your client, but do not keep it "in house" it is usually considered **cost of goods** and in **QuickBooks**® that would be a cost of goods type account. An expense of your company, but not overhead expense. You are the middle man in buying and selling the product.

Again the terminology can be confusing, as **QuickBooks**® contains both cost of goods and overhead expense accounts, which are both expenses of your company, but one is prior to your gross profit.

I have had a few clients who set up their own **Chart of Accounts** and **items**. They set their items up as **inventory**, but they only bought the goods to sell and never kept stock at their office. Their intention was completely different to what their financials showed.

In one situation with the help of my **ProAdvisor**® tech support we were able to clone the items labelled as **inventory**, make them inactive and re-create a **cost of goods** item list to match. It took the **asset** from their **balance sheet** and put the expense on their **Profit and Loss**.

So deciding if you have **cost of goods** or **inventory** is important from the start.

Items can also be made into **groups** or **assemblies**; and made up of multiple manufacturing items to make one product. For example a plumbing part, might be made up of the part, packaging, freight and service labour to put it together to make the total cost. This can be complicated, so seek advice

As outlined earlier, every transaction you make and add to your accounting software will influence your reports.

SERVICE ITEMS

What if you work in an industry that provides a service and does not need a material item or product?

First, set up a **service item** in your **QuickBooks**® and be sure you are directing or pointing the **item** to the correct income account.

You will be able to use the service item to create either/or both an **invoice** and/or a **sales receipt** in **QuickBooks**®

NO ITEMS OR PRODUCTS - COMMISSION INCOME

If you do not need to make an invoice or sales receipt, and will not be using an item or product, you might be in an industry that it will work to deposit straight into your accounting software bank account. This would mean that you would just be tracking the sales income account and not client specific, as you can with an invoice or sales receipt. The reporting features are more limited, but in some industries it works well. For example: realtors and laundromats.

As I mentioned earlier in Chapter 9, realtors or insurance agents do not always need an invoice or a sales receipt. Their income is commission and usually the expenses have already been deducted. However, it is best to include the gross and show all of their expenses as deductions, to accurately capture those expenses on their **Profit and Loss** reports.

The transaction can go directly into their deposit window of their bank account in the gross format, less their expenses.

Insurance agents are similar, receiving a monthly commission which may or may not need a sales receipt or invoice and can be directed to go into your accounting software banking account.

Keep in mind that without invoices or sales receipts your reporting features are more limited. If you need to track sales tax, this will not work.

Most businesses need what **QuickBooks**® calls **"items"** to breakdown the service they offer or to categorise a product sold or an inventory item.

Each **item** will be directed (pointing to) to an account on your **Profit and Loss** report.

Single items will most likely be directed to an income account.

Double sided items will be used to track the purchase expense and the income when sold.

SERVICE ITEMS EXAMPLES

These can be used on invoices or sales receipts.

SERVICE PROVIDED	ITEM/ PRODUCT	COST	ACCOUNT
Consulting Services	Consulting	$$	Consulting Income
Haircut – men	Haircut – men	$$	Haircutting Income
Grass cutting	Lawn cut size 1	$$	Lawn Services Income

COST OF GOODS/NON INVENTORY ITEMS

Example:

GOODS PROVIDED	ITEM/ PRODUCT	COST	ACCOUNT COG	SALE	ACCOUNT SOLD
Gift Basket	Gift Basket	$$	Goods - COG	$$	Income Gift Basket

Depending on whether the gift basket contents is **cost of goods** or **inventory** – the expense for this item from the vendor when you purchased it, (bill or cheque), would need to be accounted to either a **cost of goods** account or to a specific **inventory item**.

A gift basket **item** would most likely need sales tax turned on. Sales tax is a **preference** setting to turn on or not during your **QuickBooks®** set up process. But can be turned on later if you need it.

For reporting purposes, when sold, the gift basket **income** would go into your income account; your **cost of goods** would show the expense. If using **inventory**, your **inventory asset** would show a deduction in value on your **Balance Sheet**. Your inventory quantity would also be reduced.

This is complex, please seek guidance.

CHAPTER 13
Filing System
Making Memories

....

Before I arrived in America I made 45 photo albums and to this day, we love to look back at them and remember the memories we made. I never did get my American photos into an album and the thought of scanning is too much even right now. So, in the box they stay.

....

We talked about storing your files earlier and I will reiterate that it is very important. If you do not do it from the start it will be nearly impossible to do as time goes on and it can become a huge project.

BACK UP AND STORING YOUR DATA

The Information Technology or IT specialist suggests 3 forms of back up and I could not agree more.

- Have a physical hard drive back up or USB that you take off site.
- A cloud back up.
- Paper back up – in a file cabinet. These files will be replaced annually, but others will be permanent records.

I have had to recreate a lot of data over the years, so the need for back up and/or paper files is never far from my mind. The paper back up may be the only documentation of your transactions, if digital data is lost.

If I need to reconcile 12 months of data, I need 12 bank statements.

Bank websites only keep the statements for a few years, so be cautious. Some banks have better online systems than others.

PAPER STORAGE FILES:

I like colour coded manila files for storing paper work. I recommend four distinct categories.

1. Banking files:

- I like red or green, but plain manila is the least expensive.
- I suggest one file per month January to December.
- Store your merchant receipts (merchant copy), cheque copies, bank deposit receipts and the bank statement you have reconciled, both the bank version of the statement and your matching reconciliation report.

Anyone under the age of 25 is going to say, *no, no, I just keep it on my phone.* That is all well and good until the system breaks and you have to re-create from paper. At a minimum keep your PDF bank statements from your banking institution in your computer and scan your deposit receipts. Trust me, I have needed to reference these many times.

2. Paid Bills Files:

- These can be any colour or just manila (regular beige colour).
- Third cut files - left, middle, right tabs work well.
- Each folder should be for a different vendor, for the most common vendors.
- For example your phone company and your utility company would most likely need their own folder. If in fact you are not getting paper bills and paying online, this could be in a PDF format of storage.
- Vendor name works well for the label unless it is the type of expense.

- Office supplies or Meals and Entertainment, where no specific vendor is named, could be the labels, because you use multiple vendors.

- Include the year in your label.

- I suggest labels created from a word document, then annually change the year and add any new vendors, print and save. This is the most efficient and least expensive approach.

The banking files and the paid bills files you will want to box up and keep stored for 7 years for tax purposes. Plastic tubs are a little more expensive than cardboard banker's boxers, however they offer better protection. I had a client who had a fire from a lightning bolt; her plastic tubs protected many of her items from both fire and water damage.

3. Permanent Record Files:

These are files that usually do not change annually and you will need to keep them safe. They could be in a fire-proof safe or off site storage.

- Lease or contract for your building space.
- Annual Corporate Taxes.
- Insurance policy and declaration page.
- Equipment warranties.
- Merchant service contract.
- Bank loan documents.
- Employee records.
- Licenses.
- Online security logins and passwords (very secure).
- Leases for equipment or vehicles.

4. Reference & Resource Files:

These are files where you will store research and important reference information.

- Advertising and marketing ideas.

- Education and Training.

- Competitors Information.

- Contacts and mailing lists.

I know you can save all of this as PDF files on your computer, and you certainly can, but sometimes looking at the paperwork in your hand works best.

5. Customer Files

This varies depending on the industry:

- One manila folder per client works well.

This depends on how many projects or how long the time frame spans.

- A ring binder with dividers might work better for your industry, per client, per job.

MY FILING SYSTEM

In my business I have two types of customer files, one with notes and information about the client and projects that I might take to the client's office. The other, which holds all the paid invoices for the year. This works similar to the paid bills file and is changed out each year. My paid bills each have their own folder, except for office supplies and entertainment. Although with the new tax laws this is almost extinct. I have a separate banking folder per month, per year.

COLOUR CODING PAPER WORK

Colour coding types of correspondence is helpful too. We do not get so many faxes these days, but printing on coloured paper can be identified easily in a stack. This could be for email, or photocopies versus originals. If you are looking for an *original* it might be on one colour and the *copy* would be another.

GENERAL FILING

Within the file folder, I usually favour filing the most recent paper work to the front in any file.

Whatever your system is, it only works, if it works for you and if you use it. If you have employees or colleagues and you all follow the same steps, if should be perfect.

One assumes others know how to file, but that is not always the case. It really is unique to the individual and I have taught many a client my system and many an intern how to file in general

CLIENT EXPERIENCES

I went out of state to work for a client organising files after two businesses were sold as well as organising the home files. The same principles I have just explained worked perfectly. The business files would be boxed up and labelled. The home files were split between permanent records, banking, paid bills and reference.

I took care of the estate of my first client, the late Billy Moore, when he passed away. Knowing where all the accounts and all the passwords were was very important. I have created a spreadsheet I refer to as "The Vault" to store this information. It needs to be under lock and key or online secure, but it is very important. Nowadays of course there is an app for that.

For older file storage I suggest plastic tubs, labelled by year. You need to keep them for seven years, and then they can be shredded. However, I would encourage you to keep taxes indefinitely, especially whilst you have your business. Of course cloud based storage works well now too.

Recording Studio Filing

- One session folder for each customer. The larger clients are labelled by year, with multiple projects. Individual clients have one session folder. These include photocopies of their own financials.

- One financial folder in the accounting office with the originals, but does not have any session info. This might seem over the top, but not everyone has access to the accounting on the computer or financial files.

Again these could all be PDF's and save many trees. What works for one client, may not work for another.

Many of the financials can be stored in your accounting software, however not everyone may have access. So keeping paper or PDF files that other staff members can access is a good option.

House Builder Filing

I have worked with multiple house builders and I loved the system we had for one (thank you Debra). Each client or project had multiple different colour folders, each hanging in the same colour hanging folder until the job was complete.

- Red folder was for financial related information (invoices, payments).
- Yellow was for the contract.
- Blue was for correspondence.
- Green was for permits, licenses, etc.
- Purple for selections.
- Orange for plans.

If we opened the drawer and were looking for one of the tile selections, we would instantly be drawn to the purple folder. Both the working manila folder and its hanging partner folder matched, which makes it easy to find and re-file. When the job was complete, all manila folders were taken from the hanging folder and placed into a large manila envelope style folder with a Velcro clasp. The hanging folders were ready for the next job.

I have had other house builder clients who use a ring binder with dividers for the various parts of the job, as listed in the list previously. It also works well too.

I have clients who print one copy of every invoice and keep it in one ring binder per year. At a glance they know every invoice they have ever worked on.

A real estate agent will have a house sale folder per customer, per house sale. A mortgage broker may have the same.

CLOUD STORAGE

Your accounting system, if **QuickBooks® desktop** version is usually stored on a laptop or desktop computer, but could be stored in the cloud or on a server. I have accountants I work with, who use this system so all employees no matter their location, have access.

Many health care professionals using **QuickBooks® desktop** are required to use a server location to store their file, because of the privacy compliances.

QuickBooks online® of course is a cloud-based product and can be accessed from anywhere.

Good filing habits are a must. It is overwhelming in the beginning, but you need to start out with good intentions and try to stay on top of everything.

Keeping paper records or PDF's is actually a good thing. For tax purposes the IRS requirement is to keep back-up documentation for seven years.

As the business owner, you know what is going on, and if you took the quote, or you changed the quote. If you are not the one making the invoice, then you will need an internal system for handling this. Your employees or colleagues will need to know how to identify what is going on with a project.

As you grow your business and you will, you will need more people like you; you will need a clone. Try to create some kind of system that works for you to produce the best results, especially as you grow and you will grow.

CYBER SECURITY

Whatever system you are using, be sure to keep passwords secure and your wifi protected. Ask an IT professional for guidance.

CHAPTER 14

Profit – The Bottom Line
Home at Last

....

There is nothing like going "home." Where is home?

I have lived away from my birth country for 36 years, my children live on different continents, but my partner is by my side, home is with him.

However, in my heart, home for me will always be New Zealand, I am a very patriotic kiwi. I love to go home and enjoy the things that are uniquely New Zealand – hokey pokey ice cream, fish and chips in newspaper with pineapple fritters and of course all my family.

You will see my business name is Silver Fern Ventures. The silver fern is synonymous with New Zealand as an emblem worn on all our sports teams' apparel.

I am fortunate to have 45 first cousins, most of whom I know well and we are friends. I thank my mother for that, growing up around our extended families.

I started writing this book in 2007 in an airport lounge en-route to New Zealand and I thought I was going to finish it on board Flight 29 to New Zealand in 2017. I am now in 2018 and finally getting this out the door post tax season.

Tax time brings many new calls. It is amazing at that time of year how many people call trying to cram a years' worth of data into their systems and have it reconciled in a few weeks.

Just like the business owner who took longer to get their affairs in order, this journey for me was longer than I thought and much harder.

....

Now you are at home in your small business. The bottom line is staying on top of the paper work, customer service and making money.

If accounts are **reconciled** monthly, it is so much easier than wading through receipts and matching transactions, after the fact. More room for error.

Also at year end, if you give your accountant your *bank statements* instead of your **Balance Sheet** and **Profit & Loss** reports, be conscious that they are reviewing each transaction to create a picture of your business for the year. They will make decisions on which account to allocate or post your entries to, possibly ask you questions, and you will be paying for their time to do so. By entering your own data in **QuickBooks®** and posting to the *correct* accounts, you can run your own year-end reports and leave the accountant to do what they do best, plus possibly save yourself some money. But be sure to reach out if you need help.

Wherever possible, remember to pay yourself first.

Many business owners feel the need to bleed their company dry hoping to avoid paying tax. However when they want to sell their business, it shows no profit at all.

Try to create and read your reports to know your financial status at all times. Keep your income grouped together, accurately, then the cost of doing business, and understand your gross profit and your overhead.

From here you will see your bottom line and hopefully make a profit.

The life of the small business owner entrepreneur can be grueling; long hours, few holidays and a daily grind, but it does not need to be. I hope you have enjoyed your tour of small business and **QuickBooks®** with me.

Remember to take time along the way for you and your family. You only get one life, so make the most of it and memories along the way.

I love coaching business owners and empowering them to be armed with the knowledge they need to run a successful business. I love teaching **QuickBooks**®. You can do it!

No matter what part of the world you are in; before you go any further call me for a free consultation and I can help you with your business journey.

It's **CHeryl** with a hard **CH** *317-759-1570* or send me an email: Cheryl@silverfernventures.com.

Silver Fern Ventures

Cheryl Graham

PO Box 40605

Indianapolis, IN 46240

www.SilverFernVentures.com

Thank you for sharing my journey and good luck.

Cheryl

The Lingo

Kiwi (people): Is the nickname used internationally for people from New Zealand, as well as being a relatively common self-reference. Unlike many demographic labels, its usage is not considered offensive; rather it is generally viewed as a symbol of pride and endearment for the people of New Zealand.[10]

The name derives from a native flightless bird the kiwi which is a national symbol of New Zealand. Until the First World War the kiwi represented the country and not the people, however by 1917 New Zealanders were also being called "Kiwis" supplanting other nicknames.

Kiwi Bird: New Zealand's national bird. Kiwi or kiwis are flightless birds native to New Zealand, in the genus Apteryx family.[11]

Kiwifruit: Is a fruit native to north-central and eastern China. The fruit became popular with American servicemen stationed in New Zealand during World War II and later exported to California using the names "Chinese gooseberry" and "melonette." The first seeds were brought out of China by missionaries to New Zealand at the turn of this century. It is a popular New Zealand export today.[12]

QuickBooks® or **QBO®**: My favourite accounting software. Desktop and online versions.

Accounts Payable: Vendors you owe money to.

Accounts Receivable: Monies owed to you by your clients.

Accrual Basis: A form of accounting for reporting and tax purposes. Invoices sent but not yet paid and expenses entered, but not paid.

Balance Sheet: This is a report created from your bank account balances, liability accounts (loans & credit cards, accounts receivables, accounts payable), equity and assets.

Bank Accounts: Checking or savings accounts.

Business Tangible Tax: The tax you pay on assets of your company twice a year in May and November to your county. This could include your furnishings & office equipment.

Cash Basis: A form of accounting for reporting and tax purposes. Income collected and deposited, expenses paid.

C Corporation: A C corporation, under United States federal income tax law, refers to any corporation that is taxed separately from its owners. A C corporation is distinguished from an S corporation, which generally is not taxed separately.[13]

Chart of Accounts: This is a list of accounts to be used for all of your transactions and will formulate your Profit and Loss, and Balance Sheet reports. Business owners often refer to these accounts as categories.

Cheque: New Zealand spelling for a check.

Cost of Goods: Cost of doing business, direct costs required to create your sales or revenue income. Not your overhead expense.

Entity: This is the type of company formation you want to be. You could be working as sole proprietor, or LLC, or an S corporation, or a C corporation.

Equity: Owner's investment in his or her own company.

Estimate: QuickBooks® terminology to create the scope of a project in a financial document, an estimate or bid for a job. In **QuickBooks®** this can be transferred into an invoice.

Expense Accounts: Overhead and operation expenses.

Fixed Assets: Buildings, furniture, equipment, vehicles and any other large items owned by your company.

General Ledger: List of all your accounts with transactions.

Gross Profit: The dollar amount taking your cost of doing business from your income, before overhead expenses.

I9 Form: A document from Homeland Security to verify an employee's identification and authorization to work in the US.

Income Accounts: These show your revenue.

Interest: An expense charged on borrowed money, loan or credit card. Monthly expense added to the principal payment of a loan repayment. Tax deductible.

Internal Revenue Service (IRS): "Is the revenue service of the United States federal government."[14] The tax agency.

Inventory: Goods you sell and keep in stock, an asset of your company.

Invoice: In **QuickBooks**® terminology this is a financial document assuming you have not yet been paid for the job. It will create an accounts receivable amount due to you.

Journal Entry: A transaction to move an amount of money within your bookkeeping between accounts. Primarily used by your accountant. For example if you had equipment in an asset account (and it would be on your Balance Sheet), but your accountant thought it should be in equipment expense. He would use a Journal Entry to move the transaction.

Key Performance Indicators (KPI): A measurable value for sales targets & objectives. Reports can show what advertising works and where your budget is best spent.

Liabilities: Loans, credit card balances or payroll liabilities. Debt being carried by your business.

Limited Liability Company (LLC): "A Limited Liability Company (LLC) is a business structure allowed by state statute. Each state may use different regulations, and you should check with your state if you are interested in starting a Limited Liability Company."[15] A business entity that can be a single member or a partnership. It does not require payroll and all the profit flows to your personal income.

Member: The owner of an LLC.

Merchant services: A company that manages all your credit card payments, via a physical machine or online service for those customers who pay your business by credit card.

Non Inventory: Goods you buy to sell, but do not keep in stock, generally referred to as cost of goods - an expense.

Net Income: The bottom line, profit or losses after income and expenses have all been deducted on your **Profit and Loss** Report.

Officer: This is an official or owner of a corporation.

Paid in Capital: This is the money the owner, officer of the corporation, or member of the LLC puts into the bank account to start the business. Not to be confused with a loan from the owner.

Payroll: Owners, officers and employee are paid, and tax withholdings are sent to the federal and state government agencies. Can be prepared in house or outsourced.

Payroll Company: An outside or outsourced company that processes payroll for multiple small companies, rather than you doing your own payroll in house. (My favourite ☺).

Preferences: QuickBooks® terminology to allow the user to regulate which features they want to use within the program. You turn preferences on or off in **QuickBooks®**.

Profit and Loss: (P&L) This is a report created from your income, cost of goods and expense transactions.

Reconcile: To compare your bank statement from your bank and your accounting software. Starting balance, ending balance and all transactions in between, checked off (on paper) and definitely in **QuickBooks®** to match your bank.

Retained Earnings: At the end of the year, on your Profit and Loss report, the bottom line dollar amount will be your **net income**. This could be a positive or negative amount and will roll over to your Balance Sheet and become your retained earnings the following year.

Sales Receipt: QuickBooks® terminology for a financial document you have been paid for and the money is in your bank account. A receipt for a sale with payment.

Sales Tax: The tax you pay on materials or goods sold, paid to your state. The rate differs state to state.

S Corporation: "S corporations are corporations that elect to pass corporate income, losses, deductions, and credits through to their shareholders for federal tax purposes. Shareholders of S corporations report the flow-through of income and losses on their personal tax returns and are assessed tax at their individual income tax rates. This allows S corporations to avoid double taxation on the corporate income."[16] Officers must have payroll.

Sole Proprietor: "A sole proprietor is someone who owns an unincorporated business by himself or herself.[17] "Use your Social Security number or Tax ID.

Search Engine Optimization (SEO): Having internet buzz words and analytics imbedded into your website content to help customers find you on the internet.

Statement (Banking): This is a monthly report showing your beginning balance and ending balance, and all the transactions in between. Your bank or loan company will supply this for you to reconcile against your own records.

Statement (QuickBooks® or QBO®): A report showing transactions, including invoices and payments pertaining to a client.

Subcontractor: This is a contractor hired by a company. No taxes are withheld, but a 1099 tax form is provided in January of the following year.

Target Market: Your ideal client, the type of customer you want to work with.

Transaction Activity: This is a list of your transactions, could be debits, cheques, deposits or credit card activity, you can create reports from this, but this is not considered a statement.

Undeposited Funds: In **QuickBooks®** terminology, this is a holding account where your receive payments go until they are deposited into your **QuickBooks®** bank. It is an asset account.

UC1 and UC5A: Quarterly state unemployment reports showing wages and withholdings (Indiana).

W2[18]: Employee end of year payroll document showing total wages and withholdings. Required for employee to file taxes.

W3: IRS federal tax payroll document which accompanies the company W2's. This is a composite of all the employee W2's, showing total number of employees and annual salary. It is sent to the IRS by the end of January the following year.

W9: An IRS form the business owner gives a contractor to complete which shows the contractors name address and tax ID number or Social Security number. The contractor signs this to acknowledge they know that taxes are not being withheld.

WH3: Indiana state document showing a composite of the state and county withholdings for the year. This includes the total number of employees, salaries and withholdings, plus 1099's. It shows a breakdown per county. In Indiana this can be filed on line.

941: Quarterly Payroll report sent to the IRS showing payroll withholdings paid. This must be filed even if no payroll.

940: Annual Federal Unemployment Report sent to the IRS, to be filed by the end of January.

1099: A tax form given to a contractor showing gross payments with no tax withholdings. Due at the end of January, the year after the work was performed.

1096: The corporate form that accompanies the **1099** contractor forms, (red company copy) and is a composite of all the **1099's** listing total dollars and quantity. This is mailed to the IRS office in January.

My Clients' Thoughts – Thank you!

Empowering + Thoughtful Service

April 18, 2018

"Cheryl really cares about teaching her clients how to use QuickBooks on their own. She strives to empower you so that you feel more confident in your own abilities to use the software. Cheryl was patient with me and took the time to answer all my questions and explain things to me in depth and I never felt rushed!"

Graham Is Great!

March 19, 2018

"I am a small business owner and have had several yrs with QuickBooks desktop and recent to QuickBooks online. Before Cheryl, I hired a "self proclaimed" QB professional to do it all (office admin, taxes, QBO set up). What a mess they made! Thank the Lord for Cheryl, She walked me through step by step on how to fix and work with the new to me QBO. I now have confidence in my quick books reports again balanced to the penny! She will not rest until an issue is resolved and I will now have her do a review monthly to keep me square. With Cheryl in my corner, I can concentrate growing my business and know who to call for questions."

Remarkably Helpful

February 11, 2018

"Cheryl has taken my books (and my business) to a new level. She is everything said in these reviews and more."

Personalized service

February 5, 2018

"After almost a year of trying to figure out QuickBooks on my own, Cheryl got me moving in the right direction. She spent several hours with me at my home office helping me undo the mistakes I have made in QuickBooks. Cheryl explained things to me in a way that I could understand. We've had follow up calls and texts where she helped resolve additional problems. Cheryl really seems to care about making sure I know how to use the software to get the most out of QuickBooks. It's nice to know that if I have a problem in the future (as I'm sure I will) that I have a contact that can help me resolve any issue. I highly recommend Cheryl Graham as a QuickBooks Coach!"

Top Notch

January 23, 2018

"Cheryl helped us transition from Peachtree to QB years ago. She's always been there for us when we need her. She's professional, personable, & knowledgeable. Very good at what she does & we highly recommend her."

Easy to work with

December 5, 2017

"I own a small (but growing) real estate business and needed help getting my daily activities logged into QB Online as I work toward tax preparation. Cheryl was very patient and took extra time to learn about my business and the correct path forward for my unique situation. She also sought a second opinion when minor questions arose. After our initial meeting, we made plans to meet bi-monthly to keep me on the right track."

Small Business owner

December 1, 2017

"Cheryl was awesome to work with. She did a great job on getting my books in order and educating me at the same time. I recommend her highly."

Very helpful!!

November 20, 2017

"Cheryl was an absolute pleasure to work with. Took the time to understand our business model and then reviewed what we had in place with QuickBooks Online. We had recently lost our office manager whom ran QBO. We were completely in the dark. Cheryl took the time to sit down with us and get our accounts up to date / reconciled while identifying areas we could improve upon. Excellent instruction skills. Recommend without reservation. Thank you Cheryl!"

QuickBooks consulting

July 10, 2017

"Cheryl is a pleasure to work with. I would highly recommend her. She is very efficient at getting accomplished what I need done."

Online banking, QuickBooks, helping me to understand and get ahead of my books

March 6, 2017

"Cheryl was great to work with and helped tremendously. She's extremely thorough and did a great job getting my books in order. I have a complicated business and she was able to get things in order. I recommend her highly."

QuickBooks set up, tax set up

February 16, 2017

"I use QuickBooks Online and run my own payroll through QuickBooks Cheryl sat down with me and helped me to set up my tax accounts. We called all of the agencies to get everything set up. Cheryl is very quick to respond to my email questions and when needed helps to get me in contact with the needed person to help."

QuickBooks initiation, consulting, etc.

February 14, 2017

"I have PC Desktop QuickBooks and am not yet connected to Online banking (I need to update). I went into **QuickBooks®** upon the recommendation of my Accountant, and was given Cheryl's name and number through my check-ledger people. I have not been disappointed for 1 minute through this process! She knew I was coming into it "kicking and screaming" because I've done everything by hand for 40 years! She has been patient, and has instructed in a manner I can understand AND implement! I HIGHLY recommend that you call Cheryl Graham for your **QuickBooks®** needs and questions — she knows every little aspect of it!"

Cleaned up my 2011 QB for MAC

October 25, 2016

"I had many errors in my QuickBooks that have been sitting in open invoices for a few years, my accountant not knowing how to correct, (as I am on a Mac and he is not) I decided now was the time to get rid of all the outstanding invoices that had been paid but were somehow still showing up as being owed. Called upon Cheryl, she made an appointment to come see me within a couple of days. She was prompt, courteous, very knowledgeable and did teach me what she was doing as well as fixed my errors. I loved her and would definitely use her again. Even after she left, she called me on the phone to share something else she thought of that would affect my business and followed up with an email the next day for other stuff that I had asked her about. She knows her stuff, and I am so glad that I selected her, all the reviews were right on, which is how I determined who I would choose, thank you to all who had given comments and reviews as it certainly helps make a decision as to who to hire. I will continue to use her for a long time!"

Bookkeeping and reconciling

December 29, 2015

"Cheryl is so helpful keeping my books up to date and making sure I know what's going on behind the scenes with my business. She works hard to make sure to teach her clients so they can do for themselves and save as much money as possible. She's very detail oriented and genuinely cares for all the businesses she works for. Her knowledge has helped me better understand the money flow of my own business so I can see room for efficiency and improvement."

Month End Reconciliation and Accounting Help

December 8, 2015

"I highly recommend Cheryl Graham if you are looking for a professional to assist you or your company with your accounting needs. Cheryl has a thorough understanding of QuickBooks and has been a great help to me since I started using her. She has found areas within my business where I can save a lot of money and how I can correctly enter transactions into QuickBooks. She recently was observing some of my Merchant Services statements and saw areas where she felt I was being greatly overcharged. Through just a phone call to a professional in this business she was able to save me quite a bit of money. Cheryl is very pleasant, punctual, and easily accessible. She has made my accounting and balancing of statements much easier for me to understand. Definitely worth her weight in gold. It is an expense that I had not budgeted for but I feel she is saving me many hours of time and money."

Update to QB 2015

November 16, 2015

"We have been a client of Cheryl's since 2012 and have always come away with more than we have asked. Her knowledge of QuickBooks, business in general and her willingness to share would make her an asset to any small business. She is always available for a quick question or a more in depth project to achieve our goals."

Cleaning up a BIG QB mess

August 29, 2015

"Cheryl was absolutely fabulous! I had several different unique situations that had resulted in a big QuickBooks mess. Cheryl took the time to listen carefully to my situation and then began to help me correct it. I am a QB novice and she was very kind and patient throughout the entire project. She saved me money by calling in to QB when there was a situation that she wasn't sure about. Cheryl helped me correct my chart of accounts, my payroll liability payments that had been recorded incorrectly and especially helped me unravel problems with INtax and EFTPS. Through all of this, she kept calm and kept her sense of humor. Thank God for that! I would most definitely recommend her to anyone needing Quick Books help."

Bookkeeping instruction QuickBooks Online

October 23, 2014

"I am self-taught on QuickBooks and I don't have a background in accounting, taxes or bookkeeping but Cheryl has taught me to set up and maintain my QuickBooks so I can understand all of the time management and other important features of QuickBooks. Cheryl has a very warm and kind teaching style and is very knowledgeable when it comes to bookkeeping and QuickBooks. I never thought I would be able to use QuickBooks to run a company on my own but with Cheryl's help, I finally feel confident using QuickBooks and I see all of it's advantages. Every now and then, I meet with Cheryl just to be sure I am doing everything correctly and to get helpful tips and that just keeps me current on all of the QuickBooks updates."

QuickBooks Online

October 15, 2014

"I was starting up a business and tried to learn QuickBooks on my own as I was too busy to find someone. A business associate recommended I give Cheryl a call. She has been a Godsend. We have gone back and rectified any errors inputted by me previously and I have learned how to move forward on my own. She is very patient and well informed and not afraid to ask questions of the folks at QuickBooks if necessary. She never made me feel incompetent for my errors. I highly recommend Cheryl Graham of Victoria Grant Enterprises, Inc."

Bookkeeping

May 30, 2014

"Cheryl is fantastic! She is very detail oriented. She thinks about much more than just my books! She is like a silent business partner."

Bookkeeping

March 18, 2014

"My business wouldn't be what it is today without Cheryl. There are no words to describe the peace of mind and order she brings to me. It's always the best feeling to come into the office after she's been there knowing that everything is balanced to the penny, all bills are paid, and a detailed to do list is waiting on me. She absolutely goes above and beyond in her work. She always gives more, never less. I'm pretty sure she lays in bed at night making sure all her clients are remembering when bills are due, etc. She cares that much. Then to top it off she has this great New Zealand accent that makes bill collecting very sexy. She's 5+ stars in my book."

QuickBooks Setup and Support

August 20, 2013

"Cheryl is very professional and personable. I have been working with Cheryl for over a year now. My company works in IT Consulting and has many challenges when it comes to billing the customers. Cheryl has helped me organize my QB so it is easy enough for me to do the billing when I have time - but who has time? That's is why I hire Cheryl to assemble the invoices, reconcile my bank statements and overall, just keep me in line. One thing unique about how I am setup. She remotes in to my workstation to do the majority of the work. While "face time" with the customer goes without saying, there is no need for her to come to my office every time I need to do invoices or reconcile the accounts. While I am only one site/location, this allows a customer the flexibility of having multiple sites around the country or even around the world. As long as there is Internet access Cheryl can remote in and handle all of their locations."

QuickBooks Tutor

April 2, 2011

"Cheryl did an outstanding job of explaining in detail the QuickBooks system. It is refreshing to find such a professional."

Small business bookkeeping

March 22, 2011

"Cheryl has kept my records straight for the past 7 years. I hate that job and she has taken that burden off my shoulders."

Reviewing and making changes to our books (a church) to reflect correct profit/ loss statements and balance sheet. Would recommend her in a heartbeat. Very easy to work with and very knowledgeable.

January 22, 2011

"I would give Cheryl an overall rating of five stars. She was very knowledgeable of QuickBooks. Cheryl recognized that the church had overpaid by $13,000 in insurance premiums for our Workman's Comp insurance. She went above and beyond to ensure the church got the $13,000 refund quickly. She was also able to lower several other monthly utility payments for the church also. The money she saved us was 10 times more than made the amount we paid her in the end."

Bookkeeping

June 17, 2010

"Cheryl and I worked closely together on mutual clients for almost 7 years. She works very hard for her clients and provides excellent services. Whenever any of my clients are looking for a Quick Books expert, Cheryl is at the top of my list. I know that I can rely on her finished product when I prepare the client's tax returns. The books are always reconciled and items are categorized accurately. I do not hesitate to recommend her to anyone that would benefit from her services."

Bookkeeping, Payroll

April 22, 2010

"I have worked with Cheryl for over 10 years. Her ability combined with expertise provide me with top notch services every time. I am a CPA, and Cheryl often brings me clients information for tax work. The books are always in impeccable order, compliant and accurate. On a personal note, Cheryl is very enjoyable and easy to work with."

Bookkeeping and tax preparation

April 22, 2010

> "I have worked with Cheryl for 10 years. I find her to constantly go above and beyond for her clients. I am CPA, and when I **receive QuickBooks records** from Cheryl, they are well organized, compliant and accurate. I would highly recommend her services"

My Journey
To America

I know this is a business book, but let me give you a little insight into how I got to where I am today.

My journey to the business world began many years before arriving in America.

I came from small town New Zealand, not unlike a small town in the mid-west.

Rakaia, New Zealand

Growing up on a farm in rural New Zealand, the girls in my family were teachers. Everything changed when my father died suddenly August 28th, 1974. He was fifty-one and I was fifteen. I was living 100 miles away at a girls' boarding school, in my third year of high school.

After Dad's death I completed my term (or semester), then it was necessary for me to move back home to the family farm. I began my senior year of high school at a brand new, co-ed school and it was a very difficult transition. Before the year ended, I decided I should move to the nearest city and get a head start in the working world.

Christchurch, New Zealand

At just sixteen-years-old I boarded a bus from Rakaia (current population 1200) to Christchurch (our nearest city and 3rd largest in New Zealand) for a job interview at Jameson, Son & Anderson, an accounting firm. As I reflected later in life, I asked why had no one in my family tried to stop me, my mother or my siblings. But at the time my mother was in crisis, my older siblings gone and I appeared to be somewhat freefalling. The thought of teachers training college was a distant memory. However, I know if Dad had lived it would most certainly have been a reality.

I was excited to get my first job, working for a Chartered Accountants office and move to the city. I was going to be living with one of my favourite aunts whom I had spent many a holiday with as a child. I loved my new job, reconciling and making everything balance, and I was in my element.

However, I was also tucked away in the back office, with no client contact. I soon realised the cubicle was not for me and I missed people. My colleagues were great; Veronica and Alistair, but I needed to get out of the cubicle. So, I sought out a position with more client contact and was hired on at a car dealership. I started in the spare parts department working on both bookkeeping and spare parts products, with my colleague and lifelong friend Sarndra. Later I had the opportunity to do outside sales to the garages and services stations.

As is common with Kiwis and Aussies (Australians), travelling overseas to the UK and Europe was and still is a very popular occurrence for ages 18-26 and known as the big OE or overseas experience. Being part of the Commonwealth and wanting to see London first hand is a huge draw, and if aged under 26, the UK in turn, made it easy for us to live and work with no visa restrictions.

I was married the first time at age twenty and at age twenty three, my husband and I set off for our big OE. By then I had worked for a car dealership for seven years. We packed our house belongings into storage and headed off. We had a piece of land we were leaving, to come back and build a house on one day. We set off on June 29, 1982.

Melbourne, Australia

I had flown to Australia before, but this time it would be our first stop; in the first stage of our two year adventure. In those days you could buy a ticket that would last one year, so long as you continued in a forward direction. Our ticket was for multiple stops until we reached London. The realisation that I was leaving home for two years suddenly sunk in, I cried all the way to Melbourne, Australia.

Our plan was to travel for two years and see the world then go home to New Zealand via America. Our first year after a short visit to Melbourne we worked in Perth, Western Australia for 6 months, (we both worked at car dealerships), followed by a vacation on the beautiful island of Mauritius, in the Indian Ocean. Although we were in low budget accommodation, we shared the same beautiful beach with all the large hotels.

Johannesburg, South Africa

Time was up and our next stop was calling! We flew to Johannesburg in South Africa on January 22, 1983 where we stayed for four months, doing a few odd jobs and seeing the beautiful countryside. We were fortunate to travel from Johannesburg to Durban, to Cape Town and back, taking in the Krueger National Park. We made memories for life. Then our visa was up and it was time to move on. We made the next stop a weekend in Athens, Greece on June 4th, 1983. We took in the ruins, spent time with the locals and enjoyed the warm weather.

London, England

After almost one year we were finally arriving in the UK. We had family friends coming to meet us and the next part of our adventure was about to begin. At first we worked in a Pub in London - this was very common for Kiwis and Aussies, and that gave us live-in accommodation. We spent all our days off travelling around the country and weekends in Europe when we could swing it. After sometime we moved on to more agreeable work. I worked for a medical office on Baker Street with my colleague and lifelong friend, Carol. Later I became a courier for DHL and once again had great work colleagues including my lifelong friend Ian.

My husband's grandfather had been born in Scotland and immigrated to New Zealand. As a result of that heritage, my husband was granted a permanent visa to the UK. When our two year visa was up, we pursued the grandparent heritage visa and stayed on.

We went through periods where one or the other of us was ready to go home, but never at the same time. My husband was now working in motor racing and had found his niche. We talked about having children and decided we would have them in the UK, not wait until we went home, but were not sure it would be conducive with my husband travelling to races and no extended family support. We decided to go ahead, although as life played out, our first thoughts were accurate.

We had now moved out of London to the beautiful countryside of Surrey. In 1986 while working for DHL we welcomed Kimberley Michèle three weeks early. She was named after the diamond mines we had visited in South Africa. Her sister Stefanie Natalya Nicole arrived 21 months later. The girls went to nursery school (kindergarten) and primary (elementary) school in the UK, but as time went on we realised we would need to go home to offer them any type of life, like we had grown up with.

Brisbane, Australia

In January 1992 we put our UK house on the market and by February 1992 we were heading to Brisbane, in Queensland Australia. We took a week off to enjoy Disneyland® in Los Angeles on the way.

We absolutely loved living in Australia, the culture was similar to New Zealand, the climate was great and best of all we had some family close. We lived there for three years, but then my husband was missing his career in motor racing. So Indianapolis, Indiana was calling him and he headed to America. I remember telling my Mum, it would only be for a couple of years.

Thirty six years later, I have never been back home to live, but have gained a lifetime of experience living and working in Australia, South Africa and England, and most recently America since 1994.

Zionsville, Indiana, USA

Coming to America. My husband had come on a year ahead of the girls and me, to begin the process of getting a green card and find work.

Kimberley (9), Stefanie (almost 7) and I arrived in the United States in November 1994. It was winter in Indiana. My husband had found us a house in Zionsville and enrolled the girls in school. I had never put them on the bus for school and had only seen the yellow school bus in American movies. The first day I put them on the bus, travelling together, but getting off at two different schools was a nerve-wracking experience for us all.

Without a green card I was not able to work, but was able to volunteer at my children's school. During this first year the girls and I needed to learn how to "live in the mid-west of America."

We came from year round school so 12 weeks off in the summer was very new to us, and not knowing the need to book camps well in advance, proved challenging.

There was so much to learn and integrate culturally. For instance, I needed to learn the Pledge of Allegiance to help my children integrate into school. When seventy 9-year olds say it, it does tend to be muffled and the need for a printed copy to learn was essential.

It broke my heart that my girls were teased for their accents, a cross between British, Australian and New Zealand. But, I never knew the extent of their pain until Stefanie wrote a paper while at Indiana University about trying to integrate and talk like Americans as quickly as they could to stop the teasing. On the other hand for me, my accent proved to be beneficial and I began a new career as a voiceover talent.

In April 1995, we had our immigration meeting and said goodbye to our new friends, not knowing if we would be granted a Green Card or be on the first plane out. Our family was split up for the testing process and questioned separately, and we were fortunate to be granted a green card. I am sure post 9/11 the system is very different.

I needed to take an American driver's license test, both written and driving. I have never needed to know directions quite so well, but now all the signs noted north, south, east and west. I'd never been much of a camper, but I felt I needed a compass, it was a nightmare.

Each day as I drove out into the road I would repeat out loud, "Stay on the right," especially at traffic lights, turning on the diagonal...I think you call that catty corner (although I thought you were saying caddy), which was a new saying I learnt.

After a year we purchased a house and moved into a new neighbourhood and this is where I met my wonderful neighbour Trina. Her introduction to **QuickBooks**® has brought me to where I am today.

THE VOICEOVER INDUSTRY

As I mentioned, here my accent was unique. Through my voiceover ventures I met an amazing woman Ellie, who became my coach and critiqued my accent for the American voice over world. My name was a problem. No one in America would look at Cheryl and pronounce it with a hard CH. To make matters worse my last name was Gough at the time, which has so many variations for pronunciation.

Calling for auditions by phone made it harder than in person. I said Cheryl but they heard Carol, Jill or Sheryl. After much brainstorming we came up with the name Victoria Grant (Grant is my brother's name), only one way to spell it and although we pronounce Grant differently, US say "Gr–ant" and I say "Grah–nt", it worked better. Later I found out this was the real name of a milliner in London. We have corresponded via email and sometimes we get each other's email.

NETWORKING

My network had begun and Ellie introduced me to the late Billy Moore, a nationally known voice talent; an extremely talented and popular voice on the radio, nationwide.

Bookkeeping was not his strong suit (another term I have learnt here). Billy was quite the eccentric; a charming, sensitive and kind man. He was thankful to have me, but nervous that my new clients would replace him. That never happened; I was with him until he passed away. To this day I am still in close contact with his wife my dear friend Keka.

ACCOUNTING SOFTWARE

I enjoyed managing a business and bookkeeping. I learnt to use many different types of accounting software: Peachtree® and MYOB® (Mind Your Own Business®) – which was very popular in New Zealand. Also my New Zealand client was using the New Zealand product Xero®. But by far, living here in America my favourite was and is **QuickBooks®** and what it had to offer a new business owner.

Of course, that software has changed and morphed over the last twenty years too. As I said earlier I am not one to read the manual, so I hope I have made this easy to read and refer to.

Initially, my business network grew mostly by referrals. I was very fortunate to be referred by one client to the next client and so my business began. Also as I continued to certify with **QuickBooks®** I was listed in the directory of **QuickBooks® ProAdvisors®**, which gave prospective new clients another way to find me.

Pumpkin

Throughout my 24 years in American small business, I have had many clients' pets share my workspace, under or on the desk. Our own family cat, Pumpkin was no exception, always trying to help me organize the paper work.

My name is Cheryl Graham, I am a New Zealand born **QuickBooks ProAdvisor®**, small business consultant, entrepreneur and international voice talent.

My current practice is in Indianapolis, Indiana where I have national and international clients.

I enjoy empowering and encouraging small business owners to gain the confidence to run their business with ease.

I have had the opportunity to share my voice globally on websites, Radio and TV commercials, industry videos and "on hold" messages.

I enjoy training **Intuit QuickBooks®** accounting software as a **QuickBooks ProAdvisor®**, managing small businesses and sharing my voice around the world.

I also manage the family condo in the Florida Panhandle. I enjoy communicating with vacationers worldwide and helping them plan their next holiday.

I am married to Michael Graham, an amazing recording engineer from Indiana. Michael is also a small business owner. He shares my love of music, travel and has patiently shared this book journey. My girls are now grown; Kim currently lives here in Indianapolis, Indiana. Stefanie has been living in Sydney, Australia, but is now living in Auckland, New Zealand.

Thanks for sharing my journey.

AFTER THE TOUR

....

You took the first step by
buying this book.

Please call me for your one
hour free consultation.

It is CHeryl with a hard CH

317-759-1570

www.SilverFernVentures.com

Or email me at
Cheryl@silverfernventures.com

You can do it!

I look forward to talking to you soon.

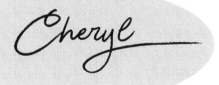

End Notes

1. IN BIZ **https://inbiz.in.gov/BOS/Home/Index** (accessed May 5, 2018)

2. IRS Website **https://www.irs.gov** (accessed May 5, 2018)

3. IRS Website **https://www.irs.gov** (accessed May 5, 2018)

4. IN-New Hire **https://in-newhire.com** (accessed May 5, 2018)

5. IN Gov **https://www.in.gov/core/** (accessed May 5, 2018)

6. EFTPS **https://www.eftps.com/eftps** (accessed May 5, 2018)

7. Indiana Tax **https://www.intax.in.gov** (accessed May 5, 2018)

8. Indiana Department of Unemployment Login
   https://uplink.in.gov/ESS/ESSLogon.htm (accessed May 5, 2018)

9. Indiana Dept of Workforce Development
   https://www.in.gov/dwd (accessed May 5, 2018)

10. Wikipedia contributors, "Kiwi (people)," *Wikipedia, The Free Encyclopedia.*
    https://en.wikipedia.org/w/index.php?title=Kiwi_(people)&oldid=826557808
    (accessed April 15, 2018)

11. Wikipedia contributors, "Kiwi," *Wikipedia, The Free Encyclopedia.*
    https://en.wikipedia.org/w/index.php?title=Kiwi&oldid=836048868
    (accessed April 15, 2018)

12. Wikipedia contributors, "Kiwifruit," *Wikipedia, The Free Encyclopedia.*
    https://en.wikipedia.org/w/index.php?title=Kiwifruit&oldid=836237387
    (accessed April 15, 2018)

13. Wikipedia contributors, "C corporation," *Wikipedia, The Free Encyclopedia,*
    https://en.wikipedia.org/w/index.php?title=C_corporation&oldid=836735143
    (accessed May 5, 2018)

14. Wikipedia contributors, "Internal Revenue Service," *Wikipedia, The Free Encyclopedia,*
    https://en.wikipedia.org/w/index.php?title=Internal_Revenue_Service&oldid=839004669 (accessed May 4, 2018)

15. Limited Liability Company (LLC)
    https://www.irs.gov/businesses/small-businesses-self-employed/limited-liability-company-llc (accessed May 5, 2018)

16. Internal Revenue S Corporation:
    https://www.irs.gov/businesses/small-businesses-self-employed/s-corporations (accessed May 4, 2018)

17. Sole Proprietor
    https://www.irs.gov/businesses/small-businesses-self-employed/sole-proprietorships (accessed May 4, 2018)

18. W2/W3/941 **https://www.irs.gov/forms** (accessed May 4, 2018)